# The Crusades

*An Enthralling Overview of an Event in Christian History That Took Place in the Middle Ages*

© Copyright 2023 - All rights reserved.

The content contained within this book may not be reproduced, duplicated, or transmitted without direct written permission from the author or the publisher.

Under no circumstances will any blame or legal responsibility be held against the publisher, or author, for any damages, reparation, or monetary loss due to the information contained within this book, either directly or indirectly.

Legal Notice:

This book is copyright protected. It is only for personal use. You cannot amend, distribute, sell, use, quote, or paraphrase any part, or the content within this book, without the consent of the author or publisher.

Disclaimer Notice:

Please note the information contained within this document is for educational and entertainment purposes only. All effort has been executed to present accurate, up-to-date, reliable, and complete information. No warranties of any kind are declared or implied. Readers acknowledge that the author is not engaging in the rendering of legal, financial, medical, or professional advice. The content within this book has been derived from various sources. Please consult a licensed professional before attempting any techniques outlined in this book.

By reading this document, the reader agrees that under no circumstances is the author responsible for any losses, direct or indirect, that are incurred as a result of the use of the information contained within this document, including, but not limited to, errors, omissions, or inaccuracies.

## Free limited time bonus

Stop for a moment. We have a free bonus set up for you. The problem is this: we forget 90% of everything that we read after 7 days. Crazy fact, right? Here's the solution: we've created a printable, 1-page pdf summary for this book that you're reading now. All you have to do to get your free pdf summary is to go to the following website:

https://livetolearn.lpages.co/enthrallinghistory/

Once you do, it will be intuitive. Enjoy, and thank you!

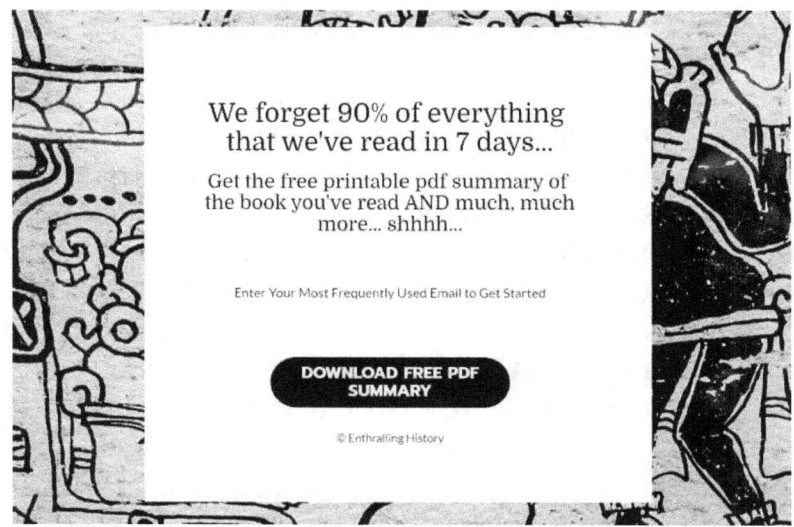

# Table of Contents

INTRODUCTION: FIGHTING ON THE SIDE OF GOD? ...... 1
PART ONE: THE CRUSADES IN THE HOLY LAND ............ 4
    CHAPTER 1: ORIGINS AND BACKGROUND ................ 5
    CHAPTER 2: THE PEOPLE'S CRUSADE AND THE FIRST CRUSADE ............ 11
    CHAPTER 3: THE KINGDOM OF JERUSALEM ............ 21
    CHAPTER 4: THE SECOND CRUSADE ............ 28
    CHAPTER 5: THE THIRD CRUSADE ............ 34
    CHAPTER 6: THE FOURTH CRUSADE ............ 39
    CHAPTER 7: THE FIFTH AND SIXTH CRUSADES ............ 44
    CHAPTER 8: THE BARONS' CRUSADE ............ 48
    CHAPTER 9: LOUIS IX'S AND PRINCE EDWARD'S CRUSADES. 53
    CHAPTER 10: THE FALL OF THE CRUSADER STATES ............ 60
PART TWO: OTHER CRUSADES ............ 63
    CHAPTER 11: THE NORTHERN CRUSADES ............ 64
    CHAPTER 12: CRUSADES AGAINST HERETICS ............ 69
    CHAPTER 13: THE ALEXANDRIAN AND SAVOYARD CRUSADES ............ 72
    CHAPTER 14: THE OTTOMAN CRUSADES ............ 76
    CHAPTER 15: THE RECONQUISTA—SETTING THE STAGE FOR THINGS TO COME ............ 83
CONCLUSION: THE LASTING LEGACY OF THE CRUSADES ......... 91

HERE'S ANOTHER BOOK BY ENTHRALLING HISTORY THAT YOU MIGHT LIKE .......................................................................... 92
FREE LIMITED TIME BONUS ................................................................. 93
APPENDIX A: FURTHER READING AND REFERENCE ..................... 94

# Introduction: Fighting on the Side of God?

*"If you are an Arabic-speaking, Greek-Orthodox going to a French school it makes you deeply skeptical if you have to listen to three different accounts of the Crusades—one from the Muslim side, one from the Greek side, and one from the Catholic side."*

-Nassim Nicholas Taleb

Over the centuries, there has been endless discussion about what started the Crusades and why they took place. In the earliest rendering of the record, the Crusades were usually explained as a cut-and-dry defensive mission to protect Christian pilgrims to the Holy Land, defend the beleaguered Byzantine Empire (modern-day Turkey), and reclaim the Holy Land, which had been lost to Christendom when Islamic forces seized it in the $7^{th}$ century.

Of course, such motivations had powerful religious overtones. However, by the $19^{th}$ century, when the zealous passion for Christianity was in decline and giving way to a host of rationalists, new interpretations were developed. It was around this time that ulterior motives for the Crusades were explored. Those who did this analysis just so happened to live during a period of great European colonization. These were the days of the "Scramble for Africa," in which almost every part of Africa (save Ethiopia and Liberia) was being rapidly colonized by European powers.

Therefore, it is unsurprising that 19th-century scholars put aside religious fervor as a motivating factor and looked at the Crusades differently. To the more rational-minded analysts, the crusaders appeared to be some sort of proto-colonizers.

But was that all the Crusades were about? Nothing more than a bloody land grab of the Middle East? *Hardly.* Anyone who takes the time to thoroughly understand what led to the Crusades and its implications will quickly realize that such rationalizations are utterly absurd.

It might be hard for us today to understand the absolute power that religion had over the masses during the Middle Ages (just as it was for folks in the 19th century), but it would leave any such analysis of the Crusades woefully inaccurate not to take such things into consideration. And considering how violent and utterly bloody the Crusades ended up being, there are those who might not want to consider religion as a motivating factor at all.

But it clearly was. One fateful day in 1095, Pope Urban II gave his clarion call to take up arms to save their Christian brothers and sisters in the East who were being encroached upon by the forces of Islam. It was not colonization that was on the minds of those who heard him. Religious fervor stirred their hearts, and as one, the gathered masses who heard the pope's rallying cry declared, "God wills it!"

For those with a keen understanding of Christian (and Catholic history, in particular), such a phrase is not a coincidence. The phrase stems from the Rule of Saint Augustine. In the 4th century, just prior to the fall of the Western Roman Empire, Saint Augustine hammered out his beliefs as to when the spilling of blood might be God's will.

Before this, Christians in the Roman Empire truly struggled with the notion of partaking in violence. This comes as no surprise since Jesus Christ advocated for nonviolence. This understandably led to pacifist-minded Christians but became a real problem after most of the Roman Empire converted to Christianity. Since the teachings of Christ promoted nonviolent methods, it became harder and harder to find soldiers willing to pick up the sword to defend Rome.

And as this ideological struggle persisted, the Roman Empire became desperate. It needed a strong army to fend off the barbarians who were growing in strength and incessantly pounding at the gates. This dilemma led Augustine to dictate the so-called "just cause" for violence, in which the people would fight because God willed it.

Yes, we can thank Saint Augustine for the rallying cry heard during Pope Urban's speech. And we can also thank him for the mentality that led Christians to believe they were somehow fighting on the side of God.

# Part One: The Crusades in the Holy Land

# Chapter 1: Origins and Background

*"There is nothing intrinsic linking any religion with any act of violence. The crusades don't prove that Christianity was violent. The inquisition doesn't prove that Christianity tortures people. But that Christianity did torture people."*

*-Salman Rushdie*

So, where did it all start? What were the origins of the Crusades? It all starts and stops with the Holy Land. It was actually a Christian Byzantine emperor who first waged a bloody war to keep the Holy Land in his possession; this was certainly a contested piece of real estate! For those of you who don't know, the Byzantines were an offshoot of the Roman Empire. After the Western Roman Empire collapsed in the 4th century, the Eastern half, which included the Levant, survived. Back then, the Byzantines didn't even think of themselves as being part of a different empire; they thought of themselves as *the* Roman Empire.

In the 7th century, the Byzantine emperor lost the Holy Land. He then waged war and recovered it. And then lost it again! The emperor's initial antagonists were not the armies of Islam (although they would come later in the same century). No, the first major opponent of the Byzantine Empire to set its eyes on Jerusalem was the Sasanian Empire, also known as the Neo-

Persian Empire. The Persians took Jerusalem in 614 CE. It is believed many Christians died in the siege, and the True Cross (the cross on which Jesus is thought to have died) was captured by the Persians. Byzantine Emperor Heraclius wrested Jerusalem back from the Persians in 630.

Interestingly enough, if we take a look back in history, this was not the first time the Persian Empire had dominion over Jerusalem. Over a thousand years prior to the Sasanian conquest, King Cyrus the Great of the Achaemenid Empire placed Jerusalem under his control. This event, which is documented in the Old Testament of the Bible, occurred in 539 BCE. Although Cyrus was in control of the region, he proved to be a benevolent monarch. He famously ended the Babylonian Captivity.

Many Jewish exiles, including the great prophets Daniel and Ezekiel, had previously been taken captive by King Nebuchadnezzar of the Babylonian Empire. After the Babylonians were trounced by Cyrus, the Jewish exiles were allowed to return and rebuild their city. Jerusalem would later be dominated by a series of empires.

In 630 CE, Byzantine Emperor Heraclius held the relic of the True Cross high over his head, declaring, "When God wills it, one man will rout a thousand. So let us sacrifice ourselves to God for the salvation of our brothers. May we win the crown of martyrdom that we may be praised in future and receive our recompense from God."

Although we view Pope Urban II's 1095 call for a religious, military campaign as the beginning of the Crusades, one could easily argue that the Crusades were put in motion when Emperor Heraclius of the Byzantine Empire declared these words and then put them into action. One could say that the religious zeal and military onslaught, for which the Crusades would be known, first came together during Heraclius's reign.

Even so, Heraclius's triumph would be short-lived. After the Byzantines drove the Persians out of the Holy Land, the Byzantine Empire and the Persian Empire fought themselves to a standstill. Both sides were thoroughly exhausted. While these two empires were trying to take a breath and recover, the forces of Islam rose up, almost entirely out of left field.

Muhammad had already perished by this time (he died in 632), but before he died, he galvanized his followers to spread Islam to non-Muslim lands. In 636, Muslim forces marched on Jerusalem, just a few years after the Byzantines had painstakingly recovered it from the Persians. Jerusalem was surrendered two years (some say one year) later, and it appears not much blood was shed. The Muslims guaranteed the Christians liberties in exchange for paying the jizya (a tax). Jews were also allowed to come live in the city again; they had not been allowed to settle in Jerusalem for over five hundred years.

The Rashidun Caliphate would also invade Persia. Because of this, Iran (the modern-day name for Persia) is predominantly Muslim instead of embracing its ancestral religion of Zoroastrianism.

Considering the rapid expansion of Islam, the natural question that arises is, why? And in particular, why did Muhammad's successors have an interest in securing the Holy Land under their dominion? First of all, one has to understand the basics of the Islamic faith. Although there is often much confusion and misunderstanding, Islam believes in the same monotheistic God as Judaism and Christianity.

However, there are certainly many religious differences. But even so, it's important to remember that, for Muslims, the term "Allah" is simply another name for the same God to whom Christians and Jews pray. Muhammad grew up in a world that was awash with religious influence, and he was fully immersed in the beliefs of both Judaism and Christianity.

After Muhammad was allegedly visited by the angel Gabriel (rendered as Gibreel in Arabic), he was galvanized to spread a new religious message. Yes, the same Gabriel that stars in the Christmas story and imparts the news of Christ's impending conception and birth to Mary is believed by Muslims to have visited Prophet Muhammad.

The Quran is basically a summary of the events that occurred in the Old Testament and New Testament of the Bible. The names are usually altered in Arabic translations—Moses is Musa, Noah is Nuh, Jesus is Isa, and so on and so forth—but the basic events and characters are the same. However, there is a big difference between Christianity and Islam, as Muhammad stated that Jesus never said he was the son of God.

The angel Gabriel supposedly imparted to Muhammad that the notion Jesus was the son of God was a gross exaggeration. Muhammad was informed that Jesus never said any such thing and that it was a claim fabricated by others after Jesus passed away. To be clear, the Quran states that Jesus was a great prophet and that he performed incredible miracles, just as the New Testament states. Yet, the Quran insists that Jesus was not the son of God.

There is actually a chapter of the Quran that addresses this issue called "The Table." The English rendering of the Arabic title sounds almost comical, and the famous verse of this chapter follows the same vein, as it states, "Isa [Jesus] son of Marium [Mary] used to eat food." This statement sounds absurd, but there is a good reason why this statement was made. It shows that Jesus was an ordinary human being who used to eat food just like everybody else.

An elaboration of this theme can be found in the Quranic verse from "The Table," Surah 5:75:

"The Messiah, son of Marium is but an apostle; apostles before him have indeed passed away; and his mother was a truthful woman; they both used to eat food. See how we make the communications clear to them, then behold, how they are turned away."

Another interesting aspect of focusing on the notion that Jesus used to eat food is the religious tradition that celestial beings, such as angels, do not eat food. The apocryphal Book of Tobit, which can be found in some Christian Bibles, delivers a tale of the angel Raphael that emphasizes this very point. It is said that Raphael disguises himself as a human and, at one point, even has to pretend to eat food to keep his disguise intact.

At any rate, the main thrust of Islam was to correct perceived "errors" such as this and to reaffirm that there was no such thing as the Trinity; there was just one sovereign God. Through the centuries, Muslims would cry out, "Allah Akbar!" ("Allah is greater!").

Muslims truly believed, just like Jews and Christians before them, that they were the ones with the true divine revelation of God. And since they claimed to believe in the same Abrahamic God as the Jews and Christians, they insisted they were the rightful inheritors of the Holy Land. They believed that Jerusalem should be under the stewardship of Muslim administrators.

Islam would indeed prove to be a powerful force to contend with. By the time of Pope Urban II's call to wrest the Holy Land back from the conquering forces of Islam, practically all of the Middle East, Near East, and North Africa were under Muslim dominion. And that was not the end of the story, for Muhammad had taught to continue the fight until the whole world belonged to Dar al Islam, or the House of Islam.

Until then, all nations outside of Muslim control or influence would be considered part of the Dar al Harb, or the House of War. The House of War was viewed as an unenlightened place of chaos; the true light of Islam could not shine there and guide the people. Those living in the House of War were seen as being hostile to the precepts of Islam. It was therefore believed that efforts should be made to allow the revelation of Islam to reach Dar al Harb as well.

Of course, most today do not take such a radical interpretation to heart. But nevertheless, it simply can't be denied that Muhammad's successors and their huge armies pushed forward with the expansion of Islam. They wanted to create an empire that was safe for Muslims to practice their faith and also spread the faith to others. In their minds, everyone should hear about the way of Allah since it was simply the right way to live. This might sound similar, as this was also how Christians viewed their religion at the time.

And so, the Islamic expansion continued. Islamic corsairs from North Africa landed in Spain and took over much of the Iberian Peninsula. Muslim conquerors then pushed on into France. Sicily was seized as well. It's often forgotten how much Christian Europe was on the defensive at the time. Considering all of this, the truth is if the pope had not galvanized the forces of Christendom to stand up to the encroaching armies of Islam, Europe stood a good chance of being overrun.

Christians had long been on the defensive when it came to the Muslims, but with Pope Urban's call for a crusade against Islam in 1095, they would finally go on the offensive. So, along with the pretense of defending the Byzantines and recovering the Holy Land, it wouldn't be too hyperbolic to say the defense of Europe was at stake as well. Even though the Holy Land and the Byzantine Empire would ultimately be lost, Spain, parts of France, and Sicily were recovered for Christendom. Prior to Pope Urban's address, these regions were in a perilous state.

Pope Urban II was not the first pope to consider calling a crusade. His predecessor, Pope Gregory VII mused about as much in 1074 upon seeing the perilous condition of the Mediterranean, declaring that it was time for Christendom "to take up arms against the enemies of God and push forward even to the Sepulcher of the Lord under his supreme leadership." No matter what anyone might say about the later abuses and motivations of the crusaders, there can be no doubt that it was Islamic encroachment that triggered the initial call to arms.

By the time the First Crusade was called, the Muslim forces had been steadily chipping away at the Christian Byzantines in the East. The Byzantine emperor's request for aid against this threat would morph into a larger call to bring glory to Christendom and potentially take back the birthplace of Christianity itself: the Holy Land.

Although some other ulterior motives and events drove the Crusades forward, fighting against Islamic encroachment was indeed the fundamental origin of the Crusades. As the forces of Islam pushed more and more into Christian lands, there were really only one of two possibilities: either the Christian nations crumbled and eagerly submitted to Islam, or a cataclysmic holy war would be triggered. As history can attest, it was the latter that happened.

# Chapter 2: The People's Crusade and the First Crusade

*"If there ever was a religious war full of terror, it was the Crusades. But you can't blame Christianity because a few adventurers did this."*

*-Moustapha Akhad*

Even before the first professional armies of Europe descended upon the Holy Land, the first to arrive on the scene were not from the knightly or noble classes. Rather, a rabble of impoverished masses led by an itinerant preacher known as Peter the Hermit made their way eastward. This massive tidal wave of peasants would become known as the People's Crusade. In this unofficial crusade, which had been inspired by Pope Urban II's call to arms, the words of a passionate preacher galvanized the poor and huddled masses of western Europe to take up the cross and "fight the good fight."

Just imagine this monk standing around in the middle of a poor medieval village, speaking of how all good Christians needed to take up the struggle against evil. It might be hard for us to fathom it today, but back then, people took the words of this firebrand preacher seriously. Peasants literally dropped everything they were doing to follow this "Pied Piper" wherever he led them.

Farmers left the fields, and bakers left their bread just to follow Peter the Hermit and take on the "infidels" in the Middle East. Even though the pope had ordered the professional soldiers of Europe to take time to prepare themselves before disembarking on the prearranged launch date of August $15^{th}$, 1096, those who participated in the People's Crusade were so eager and zealous that they made practically no preparations whatsoever.

They set off of their own accord shortly after the pope's initial call to arms in November 1095. This unorganized mob caused trouble wherever it went. As they passed through central Europe, the People's Crusade viciously assaulted Jewish settlements simply due to the fact that they were of a different faith. This group of marauders also failed to bring adequate supplies with them, so banditry took place, with the people roving the countryside and stealing whatever they could.

Such things hardly seem Christian, yet terror was inflicted upon countless villages as the People's Crusade traveled through Europe. When they reached the Balkans and neared the Byzantine Empire's borders, they caused even more trouble by harassing the locals there. This led to several outright clashes with Byzantine authorities, but somehow, the group eventually made it to the Byzantine capital of Constantinople. The Byzantine emperor, Alexius I Komnenos, quickly washed his hands of them and sent them on to Asia Minor, which was then occupied by Turkish Muslims.

In the vicinity of the once-great Byzantine (but, at that time, Turkish-occupied) city of Nicaea, Sultan Kilij Arslan I of the Seljuk Empire made short work of Peter the Hermit's would-be crusaders. Although the European peasants were good at harassing unarmed villagers, this unsavory group proved entirely ineffective against the professional forces of the Turks. Most of the poorly trained mob of people did not have armor, and some did not even have proper weapons. Imagine folks wielding pots, pans, and broomsticks against a Turkish scimitar! With this image in mind, you can easily understand what an absolute disaster this battle was.

The Turks themselves must have been astonished at the comic absurdity of this bizarre spectacle, of this ragged band of people who had suddenly dropped in on them. At any rate, the People's Crusade was almost entirely annihilated. The First Crusade—as in the first *official* crusade—would be another matter entirely. The people who fought in the First Crusade took their time to prepare. Their campaign would not be launched until the summer of 1096. More importantly, this crusade was made up of professional soldiers

Let's briefly review what led to the First Crusade. In November 1095, in Clermont, France, Pope Urban II gave an impassioned speech to a gathering of French nobility and church clergy, highlighting the perceived threats of Islam and the need to defend the Christian Byzantine Empire and rescue the Holy Land. Breaking with custom, the pope delivered his speech in French rather than Latin. It was a smart move; by speaking in French, Urban was assured that all of those present understood him and the gravity of the situation.

To hear the pope speaking in the local French vernacular would have really helped drive his points home to the audience. He listed a whole litany of grievances that the "enemies of Christianity" had committed. Pope Urban II was known to be an eloquent public speaker, and he was able to perfectly highlight the perceived enemy while calling for a so-called "Truce of God" to unite fellow Christians.

Prior to Urban's call for the First Crusade, there were seemingly non-stop squabbles and skirmishes among Christian principalities. Also, in 1054, the Eastern and Western Churches split away due to differences in doctrine and other issues. For instance, there was a disagreement over the pope's infallibility or whether to use leavened or unleavened bread in ceremonies. These were just two of the items on the churches' long list of grievances with each other. The Great Schism rocked the Christian world, and the split between the Eastern and Western Churches still exists today. It is possible that Urban was hoping to help heal the split and bring the two churches closer together.

Pope Urban II pleaded with the nobles before him to put their differences aside and come together for a common cause and to take a stand against the forces of Islam. As Pope Urban II put it, "Let those who have been accustomed to make private warfare against the faithful carry on to a successful conclusion of war against the infidels, which ought to have begun ere now. Let those who once fought brother and relative now fight against barbarians as they ought."

As it turns out, the crusaders were quite fortunate. As they were putting aside their differences by enacting the "Truce of God," the dominant forces of Islam were, for the most part, in disarray. The Turks, in particular, had been facing a succession crisis ever since the Turkish warlord Sultan Malik Shah passed away in 1092. For the next few years or so, the Middle East would see near-constant fighting between the competing factions of successors who fought for dominance.

In truth, this was not unknown in the West. Pope Urban II had been informed of as much by Byzantine Emperor Alexius Komnenos at the Council of Piacenza in March 1095. The Byzantine emperor had pleaded for military support against the Turks, viewing the sudden dissension in their ranks as a prime opportunity for him to regain lost ground in Asia Minor. Little did Emperor Alexius know that the pope would issue an all-out impassioned plea to not only aid the Byzantines against the Turks but also potentially seize the Holy Land itself.

And the pope's call to arms had the desired effect. Soon, the whole crowd was shouting as one, "Deus lo vult!" ("God wills it!") Those who heard Urban's words were so inspired that they began tearing cloth into makeshift crosses to place on their backs to symbolize their "taking up the cross" to fight for the Holy Land.

The pope even sweetened the deal by offering exemptions from time in Purgatory. According to Catholic belief, an in-between realm called Purgatory exists. It is believed that many will bide their time there before they are able to go to heaven.

But how could the pope even promise such a thing? Well, in the Bible, Christ proclaims to Peter (whom the Catholics cite as the first pope) that "whatever you bind on Earth will also be bound in heaven, and whatever you loose on Earth will be loosed in Heaven." The Catholics believe the pope was given the "keys" to Earth and heaven. Catholics had no issue with popes excommunicating believers; lessening time in Purgatory would be under their purview as well.

It was no small thing for the pope to offer to use his power to lessen one's stay in Purgatory. Although we might be tempted to scoff at such a thing today, such a gesture would have been quite meaningful to Christian believers of this time period. Why wouldn't they jump at the chance to be with God and their loved ones sooner?

In all, it is estimated that some sixty thousand troops were assembled. They were led by European nobles, which included Henry, the brother of King William II of England, and Hugh of Vermandois, the brother of King Philip I of France. The Crusades would establish a long tradition of a king's brother going to war. It was simply far too risky for a sitting monarch to head to war in the Middle East, although it was not unheard of, as we will see later on.

This group of crusaders made their way to the Byzantine capital of Constantinople (modern-day Istanbul) in the summer of 1096, making it to their destination in the early months of 1097 (some began to arrive in November 1096).

They would remain in Constantinople for some time before setting off once again that fall. There was logistical maneuvering to work out, and adequate supplies needed to be obtained. The Byzantine emperor was genuinely grateful to have—if anything else—a major distraction to unleash upon his enemies. He duly provided the crusaders with whatever they needed.

Interestingly enough, the crusaders made a solemn pledge to Alexius Komnenos that they would return any and all territory that had formerly belonged to the Byzantine Empire. This was a rather curious pledge to make since many of the former Byzantine territories, including the Holy Land itself, had been lost long ago. Additionally, keeping this pledge would prove far more difficult than giving it.

At any rate, the crusaders set off for their first real engagement: recovering the city of Nicaea, which had been seized from the Byzantines some twenty years prior. This was the same Nicaea where the People's Crusade (led by Peter the Hermit, who was still alive) met its terrible end at the hands of the Turkish warlord Kilij Arslan.

Fortunately for the crusaders, Kilij Arslan was away on other business at the time, which gave the Europeans an edge over their unprepared opponents. Even without this advantage, this Crusading force was entirely different from Peter the Hermit's force. The crusaders were properly trained and armed; they were an efficient fighting machine. If any of the Turkish defenders who slew Peter the Hermit's followers thought that these outsiders would be just more of the same, they were sorely mistaken.

The crusaders also had the benefit of actively coordinating with Byzantine troops. During the course of the battle, Emperor Alexius made the wise decision to put his naval craft in range of Lake Ascania near Nicaea, effectively blocking off any potential reinforcements. Soon, the crusaders were attacking their opponents on all sides.

Utterly defeated, the Seljuk Turk forces that survived the melee were forced to surrender. Emperor Alexius, who was, of course, much more well-versed in the politics of the region, took over the negotiations. He oversaw the repatriation of Nicaea to the Byzantine Empire. Although Alexius was successful in ensuring that Nicaea was returned, it would not be long before the crusaders began to go back on their pledge of returning lost Byzantine lands.

In many ways, such things are understandable, at least considering them from the viewpoint of the crusaders. Back in those days, land was everything. To be a landed noble meant to be secure. These men had traveled far and had fought hard—save for the most religious—and many undoubtedly began grumbling that they were getting the raw end of the deal. They probably began to question the merits of fighting and dying to restore land to a foreign emperor to whom they had no real allegiance.

Thus, one can easily see why some of them might have begun pushing for some sort of reward of their own. Nevertheless, they allowed the Byzantines to continue guiding them along. They ultimately headed to the mountains of Cappadocia, where they were able to link up with the Armenian resistance. From here, they planned their next major objective: seizing the fabled city of Antioch in the northwestern Levant.

The crusaders reached the gates of Antioch in October 1097. They found themselves in an advantageous position, as they had a constant supply line from their Armenian allies. Even better, an English-led fleet had managed to secure Antioch's port of St. Symeon and was able to open up a direct line to the Byzantine-controlled island of Cyprus.

These open routes of access allowed precious supplies important for siege warfare, such as timber, to be obtained. The supplies were funneled by Genoese sailors, who sailed across the Mediterranean. But even with all of this support and good fortune, the conquest of well-fortified Antioch would be a difficult task. By December, the crusaders were low on food and morale.

A mystic named Peter Bartholomew entered the picture in a big way. Peter was among the main crusader force at Antioch. He gained widespread attention in the camp after he claimed to have had a vision that led him to eventually discover the Holy Lance. This artifact has a long and controversial history. The relic is said to have been the spear that pierced Christ while he was nailed to the cross. It was later known as the Spear of Destiny. There is a whole mythic backstory behind the spear that suggests that whoever has this relic is destined to conquer.

Once the spear was discovered (or perceived to have been discovered, as we don't know for certain if it was *the* spear that pierced Christ), the crusaders were greatly inspired. About ten days later, they finally took the city in June 1098.

In the meantime, the crusaders became angered with the Byzantines. The Byzantines learned the crusade was a lost cause and that the crusaders were on the verge of defeat from a defector from the crusader ranks, Stephen of Blois. It was not true, but the Byzantines accepted this pessimistic and dire forecast and ceased lending aid to the crusaders.

The crusaders nominated their own supreme leader, Bohemond, Prince of Taranto (a Norman principality that was part of the larger Kingdom of Sicily). Since the Byzantines proved so fickle and had turned their backs on the crusaders, Bohemond refused to repatriate Antioch to the Byzantine Empire. Instead, it became part of what would later be known as the Crusader States.

The crusaders hunkered down in Antioch to recover before marching to the gates of Jerusalem, a feat that was reached on June 7th, 1099.

The crusaders knew they were fighting a holy cause, but seeing Jerusalem must have inspired some awe in them. It is easy to imagine the Christians taking a breath and realizing just what they were taking part in. It is said that the following day, priests actually led a barefoot procession around the walls of the city while holding religious relics aloft. This was likely done in imitation of the biblical story about the walls of Jericho. In that story, the high priest led the Israelites around the walls of Jericho just prior to laying siege to the city. According to scripture, the walls miraculously came tumbling down. In the Old Testament, Jericho was one of the first major engagements the children of Israel faced as they established themselves in the "Promised Land."

The crusaders read the biblical stories and hoped for the same outcome. But unlike the biblical description of what happened in Jericho, once the crusaders finished circling the walls of Jerusalem, the city walls still stood as strong as ever. The taking of this fortified city would be no easy task.

Due to deaths and desertions, the crusader force had been whittled down to a fraction of what it had been at the outset. Yet, all the same, a core group of diehard warriors would fulfill the pope's call to seize the city of Jerusalem for Christendom. Interestingly enough, as the Christian crusaders stood just outside the gates of Jerusalem, the Muslim governor of the city, Iftikhar ad-Dawla, issued an order to have all Christian residents kicked out of the city.

Considering the violence of the period, it is probably commendable that the governor did not have the Christians killed outright. But his bid to remove them surely had ulterior motives all the same. The governor probably feared the local Christians might aid the crusaders from within. Just imagine how easy it might have been for a Christian on the inside to open a hidden gate and invite the Christian warriors inside the walls. This fear could have been a motivator for the governor to get the Christians out ahead of the siege.

He also might have wanted to use the expulsion of the local Christians as a major distraction since it created an immediate humanitarian problem for the crusaders. As happy as they might have been to see their Middle Eastern brothers and sisters of the faith, they now had to share their already limited resources to feed the exiled population. The crusaders made do as best they could and settled down right outside the walls of that long-sought-after city.

The governor's decision to expel the Christian citizens would ultimately backfire on the city's defense. A Christian from Jerusalem known as Blessed Gerard, who managed a hospital of sorts for the sick in Jerusalem, came into contact with crusader commanders and offered up his services. Gerard had intimate knowledge of the city's defenses and convinced the crusaders that he could aid them in their siege.

With Gerard's help, the crusaders were able to pinpoint the most vulnerable points of Jerusalem's defenses. The crusaders constructed three siege towers and used them to exploit these vulnerabilities. Nevertheless, the defenders of the city fought back hard and managed to take down two of the siege towers. The third was expertly maneuvered to one of the main gates of the city, giving the crusaders access. They successfully scaled the walls on July 15th, 1099. After a bitter, bloody struggle inside the city, Jerusalem was under crusader control.

By all accounts, what followed next was a terrible, bloody massacre. The crusaders roamed the streets, killing all non-Christians they came across. It is said the streets literally ran with blood. As contemporary chronicler William of Tyre put it, "It was impossible to look on the vast numbers of the slain without horror; everywhere lay the fragments of human bodies. Still more dreadful was it to gaze upon the victors themselves, dripping with blood from head to foot. Then, clad in fresh garments with clean hands and bare feet, in humility they began to make the rounds of the venerable places which the Savior had deigned to sanctify and make glorious with His bodily presence."

The only ones who were spared were those holed up in the city's fortified citadel. One of the leading crusaders, Raymond of Saint Gilles (also known as Raymond IV, Count of Toulouse), opened up a dialogue with those inside and promised them safe conduct out of the city if they surrendered. Despite all of the previous bloodshed, Raymond kept his word. Once the defenders of the citadel put down their arms, they and the few survivors they were defending were allowed to leave Jerusalem in peace.

As terrible as it all was, the Christian crusaders truly believed that God had willed them to take the Holy Land and seize the city for Christianity. They believed they were the instruments of God's wrath. Immediately after the killing of non-believing infidels, the crusaders donned their robes and went on a peaceful pilgrimage to the holy sites, a journey they had long yearned for. It might be hard for us to fathom such things today, but this sort of compartmentalization of actions was quite common during the time of the Crusades.

The crusaders were able to kill for what they believed was a just cause and then put on robes of penance as they visited the venerated sites. Even so, it could very well be that some suffered from what today would be termed "PTSD." As much as they kept telling themselves that God willed it and that they were excused in their actions, many undoubtedly woke up in the middle of the night with nightmares over some of the things they had done.

The objectives of the First Crusade had been achieved. Ironically enough, the man who had instigated all of this to occur in the first place—Pope Urban II—perished two weeks prior to Jerusalem being seized. Pope Urban II did not get the chance (at least on this side of eternity) to see his vision fulfilled. Nevertheless, the wheels had been set in motion, and the subsequent course of history had been determined.

# Chapter 3: The Kingdom of Jerusalem

*"In the Crusades, getting the Holy Land back was the goal, and any means could be used to achieve it. World War II was a Crusade. The firebombing of Tokyo by Doolittle and the carpet bombing in Germany, especially by the British, showed that."*

*-Stanley Hauerwas*

The crusaders who conquered Jerusalem would soon find out that, in many ways, conquering was the easy part. It was rebuilding the city and holding it that would prove far more difficult. From the outset, there were problems to be addressed. The city walls had been pulverized during the crusader assault, which left the new residents vulnerable to attack. The population of the city was also quite small and quickly dwindling.

Due to the massive slaughter, the local population had been greatly reduced, and the crusaders could not be depended upon to stay. Many had families back home and were eager to leave the Holy Land as soon as possible. Fairly soon after Jerusalem had been conquered, which had been taken at the cost of much blood and treasure, the city was beginning to look more like a ghost town than the center of the Christian faith.

There were barely enough people to man strategic towers and gates, which was necessary for the overall security of Jerusalem. It didn't take much for thieves to waltz right through a crack in the wall in the dead of night. As such, instances of robbery became quite common.

As chronicler William of Tyre explained, "Even within the city walls, in the very houses, there was scarcely a place where one could rest in security. For the inhabitants were few and scattered and the ruinous state of the walls left every place exposed to the enemy. Thieves made stealthy inroads by night. They broke into the deserted cities, whose few inhabitants were scattered far apart, and overpowered many in their very own houses. The result was that some stealthily, and many quite openly, abandoned the holdings which they had won and began to return to their own land."

The crusader-occupied city of Jerusalem desperately needed an infusion of new blood to make up for all the blood that had been lost. So, European pilgrims were incentivized to come to the Holy Land to not only visit but also become permanent residents. The rich and fertile lands were set at an attractive price and were easy to obtain. However, efforts like this have often led to the Crusades being likened to an early attempt at colonization. It is understandable why such a parallel might be made, but the conditions were decidedly different.

Most of those who came to the Holy Land were just passing through and had no intention of settling long-term there. Rather than being colonists intent on putting a stake in the ground, farming, and settling the community, these were primarily religious pilgrims whose main objective was to visit the religious sites, pray, and then go home. Some would end up staying, but many would not.

Along with bringing in some new Christians to the city, the city authorities tried to keep the old Christians—such as Eastern and Armenian Orthodox followers—from leaving. The authorities established the absentee landlord law. This law was an interesting legal development, as it dictated that anyone who owned land could not rent it out and then move away. The legislation stipulated that any landowner had to reside in the city at least once a year, or their property would be considered up for grabs.

These measures were helpful, but the biggest problem the residents of Jerusalem faced was always going to be the threats that confronted them just outside of the city walls. Traveling from Jerusalem to other places in the Levant was always an enterprise filled with considerable risk since there were bandits and hostile armies with which to contend. One never really knew what might happen to them if they stepped outside the walls of Jerusalem.

This fact was clearly demonstrated by an incident that occurred shortly after the city's conquest was complete. On Easter Sunday, a group of some seven hundred Christian pilgrims, who were intent on visiting the Jordan River to observe the famed place where Jesus was baptized, were ruthlessly assaulted. Around three hundred pilgrims were murdered, and about sixty of them were taken as prisoners. They likely suffered a horrendous fate, as it is believed they were sold as slaves. Roughly half survived, fleeing in terror back to the safety of Jerusalem.

The dangers of traveling from one spot in the Holy Land to another led to the establishment of special monastic orders of knights, which would serve as official escorts and protect the Christian pilgrims. The Knights Templar became one of the main honor guards, as they were utilized to escort civilians from one place to another. The Knights Templar may not have been large in number, but they were fierce and efficient to such a degree that just a small group was capable of taking on hundreds of opponents at one time.

The Knights Templar are believed to have been officially founded in 1119 in the early years of the Kingdom of Jerusalem (founded in 1099). The order was established by a French nobleman named Hugues de Payen. The official name of the group was The Poor Fellow-Soldiers of Christ and of the Temple of Solomon. (A mouthful, to be sure!) The name was taken from the Temple Mount in Jerusalem, where the Knights Templar made their headquarters. The mention of being poor is in reference to this monastic order's vow of poverty.

And in the early days, the Knights Templar certainly lived up to this pledge. The knights had a communal lifestyle and dressed in modest, monkish clothing (at least when not regaled in battle armor). Once the Templars became the bankrollers of the Middle

Ages, their status would change, although their vows stayed the same.

Although the Knights Templar would become the most famous of the monastic orders, they were preceded by others. Most notably, there was the Knights Hospitaller, an order that was officially founded in 1099, prior to the Templars. However, they had been operating before the founding of the Kingdom of Jerusalem itself. The Knights Hospitaller set up hospitals and shepherded pilgrims to religious sites before Jerusalem was taken. It was only at the dawning of the 1100s that the order took on a more militaristic makeup.

Another order that predates the Knights Templar is a little-known monastic order called the Order of Saint Lazarus. This order, which would later become more commonly known as the Leper Knights, actually began its existence as a hospital for lepers. Some believe this treatment facility actually predated the Islamic conquest of Jerusalem, going all the way back to Roman rule. It is believed the hospital was founded by the Roman Catholic icon Saint Basil. However, the order didn't begin until later, as it was initially a Knights Hospitaller order.

Considering the constant need for warriors, knights afflicted with leprosy were not ordered to retire; instead, they joined the Order of Saint Lazarus. They continued to provide their services even though they were effectively isolated from the rest of the community, relegated to living just outside the gates of Jerusalem in the leper hospital.

At any rate, these Leper Knights were most certainly a fearsome sight. Just imagine a group of knights on horseback, wrapped in bandages that barely hid their terrible open sores, suddenly charging down on you. These guys were virtually immune to pain due to their deadened nerves. As such, the frantic blows of the enemy were barely even felt. Known as the "living dead," these ferocious warriors would raise their broadswords high over their heads and tear their opponents to shreds with no fear whatsoever for their own safety.

These men had the bravery of those who already knew their time was short and figured they might as well go out fighting for what they sincerely felt was a good cause (whether we agree with such notions today or not). All of this made them incredibly formidable fighters. The Leper Knights were dreaded by all, not only because of their ferocious capacity to fight but also out of fear of catching leprosy from being in close contact with them.

There were many other monastic orders that were tasked with providing extra security for those traveling back and forth in the Kingdom of Jerusalem. They also covered the security details for any pilgrims visiting from Europe. But while security is important for a kingdom, a kingdom also needs a king. Surprisingly, the early crusaders were hesitant to take on such a title. Their reverence for Jerusalem was so great that it seemed arrogant to be called the "king of Jerusalem."

This attitude led Godfrey de Bouillon, the first man charged to be the administrator of Jerusalem, to refuse the title altogether. Even though he technically was the first king (he was made ruler on July $22^{nd}$, 1099), he insisted on being referred to as simply the "Defender of the Holy Sepulchre." This title was in reference to the Church of the Holy Sepulchre, which was greatly revered by the Christians. It wouldn't be until December $25^{th}$, 1100, that the Kingdom of Jerusalem would be overseen by a king. On that date, Godfrey's brother, Baldwin, Count of Edessa (another Crusader state), was crowned.

Godfrey de Bouillon had suffered from a long illness the previous summer. It took some debate to decide who should rule next, but the honor ultimately fell upon Godfrey's brother.

Initially, the Kingdom of Jerusalem was a very basic patchwork of cities that the crusaders had taken. Under Baldwin's reign, this patchwork would expand into a true kingdom, which would make up roughly the boundaries of the modern state of Israel, plus the southernmost regions of Lebanon. Baldwin seized Acre in 1104 and then charged north all the way to Beirut in 1110.

Under the administration of King Baldwin, the population of Jerusalem swelled to a much more comfortable number, at least when compared to the sparsely populated region that existed before. The Kingdom of Jerusalem was fortified into a well-defended Christian state. King Baldwin had already helped shore up relations with the local Christians in the Middle East by marrying an Armenian woman named Arda. This move especially helped him shore up strong relations when he oversaw the County of Edessa, which had a strong Armenian presence.

However, Baldwin was not the most faithful husband. Once Arda had served her purpose, he married a new wife: Adelaide del Vasto. Adelaide was a rich scion of Sicily, so she was a tremendous boon to Baldwin's floundering resources. However, Baldwin was still married to Arda when he married Adelaide. He eventually decided to send Adelaide packing in 1117, upsetting her son, Roger, who was the count of Sicily. Roger would later become the king of Sicily, and even then, he refused to support the Kingdom of Jerusalem.

Baldwin would pass away the following year, 1118, without providing any heirs to take the throne. The crown was initially offered to Baldwin's brother, Eustace III, but Eustace had other plans. So, the crown was handed over to Baldwin of Bourg instead.

The new king was sworn in on Easter Day in 1118. He was crowned by the patriarch of Jerusalem and officially became King Baldwin II of Jerusalem. Baldwin II proved himself to be a formidable defender of the realm. He stood up to incursions from both the Seljuk Turks and the Fatimids of Egypt. However, Baldwin would pay the price for his boldness when he was taken prisoner and captured by his opponents at the infamous Battle of Ager Sanguinis in 1119.

This battle saw a whole host of crusaders, who had been cobbled together in Antioch, annihilated almost to the man. In the aftermath of this terrible exchange, Baldwin was taken hostage. Incredibly enough, King Baldwin would not be released until 1124. It is not entirely clear what Baldwin had to endure during his captivity, but he would prove himself still fit to be king after he was released. The following year, he led his forces to victory in the Battle of Azaz in 1125.

During the reign of King Baldwin II, the formidable monastic order of knights known as the Knights Templar was established. Baldwin II had four daughters, and upon his passing, his oldest daughter, Melisende, would be crowned as the next ruler of the Kingdom of Jerusalem. She would go on to marry Fulk V, Count of Anjou. Fulk proved to be an able leader, but after his abrupt passing in 1143, the Kingdom of Jerusalem faced its first real loss. The County of Edessa was lost to Zengi, an Islamic warlord from Mosul.

The loss of Edessa would lead to the Second Crusade. We will dive more into the Second Crusade in the following chapter, but suffice it to say, it did not go well. At any rate, Fulk and Melisende had a son named Baldwin (later known as King Baldwin III). Baldwin III would perish without an heir, and his brother, Amalric, would ultimately ascend to the throne.

Amalric's son—yet another Baldwin—succeeded him. Baldwin IV, the Leper King, as he would later be known, would not have an easy time with things. Just as his moniker implies, he had leprosy. But despite his terrible sickness, Baldwin IV was a stable hand at the helm. After his death, the Kingdom of Jerusalem, which had long been besieged by adversaries, would fall once again.

# Chapter 4: The Second Crusade

> *"The first two crusades brought the flower of European chivalry to Constantinople and restored that spiritual union between Eastern and Western Christendom that had been interrupted by the great schism of the Greek and Roman Churches."*
>
> -Joseph Jacobs

The Second Crusade was a direct call to action after the loss of the Crusader principality of Edessa. After Edessa fell to Islamic forces in 1144, Christians felt compelled to recover it. It had been some fifty years since the First Crusade successfully wrested much of the Holy Land from Islamic control. The first loss of Crusader land came as quite a shock. As soon as word reached western Europe, the situation was presented as a calamity of epic proportions and one that all of Christendom had to address.

On December 1st, 1145, Pope Eugenius III issued the official call for a crusade, encouraging Christians to "take up the cross" and to "live up to the deeds of their forefathers" who had seized the Holy Land during the days of the First Crusade. The pope was basically chiding the new generation of potential warriors not to become ill-begotten stewards and lose the precious lands their ancestors had fought so hard to secure.

This papal call for a crusade was perhaps not quite as attractive as the first since a heavy dose of self-recriminating guilt and heroic ambition laced the dialogue swirling around the Second Crusade. But it was indeed successful enough to at least get the point across. The papal promise to hold up those who died as martyrs, guaranteeing them "a place in heaven," certainly didn't hurt either. For the deeply religious of the Middle Ages, such sentiments meant everything.

And as soon as that mindset is understood, one can understand why folks in western Europe would travel thousands of miles to risk life and limb in the Middle East. The notion that one was "fighting the good fight" and struggling on the side of God was an incredibly powerful motivator for both Christian and Muslim armies.

Back in Europe, King Louis VII of France had been actively recruiting troops on his own. Louis made his own personal call to action around Christmastime, shortly after the pope's address. A popular French theologian, Bernard of Clairvaux, aided the French king. Louis proved pivotal in gathering professional soldiers, so much so that the pope was inspired to issue a renewed call for a crusade on March 1$^{st}$, 1146, in which he specifically designated Bernard of Clairvaux as a spokesman for the cause.

Bernard gave a powerful sermon on the matter on March 31$^{st}$ (Easter Sunday) to a group of gathered faithful in Vézelay, France. Bernard's sermon, rather than the pope's personal call for a crusade, truly galvanized the masses. The pope accused his audience of letting past conquests slip out of their grasp. Bernard spoke in glowing terms of blessing and hope, preaching how blessed this new generation of Christians was to have the opportunity to seek "such splendid spiritual riches" in their quest to rescue the Holy Land. His sermon was a much more positive and attractive variation of the pope's call to arms and seemed to stir the hearts of those who listened to it.

After Bernard's powerful oratory, the king of France and his queen, Eleanor of Aquitaine, made a pointed show of humility, bowing down before Bernard as they symbolically "took up the cross." Shortly thereafter, King Louis VII led the crusaders from France to Germany. Once in German lands, Bernard gave his blessings to the German king, Conrad III, as well as his nephew (and future Holy Roman emperor), Frederick Barbarossa. It has been said that Conrad was initially hesitant to participate in the Second Crusade, but the words of Bernard of Clairvaux convinced him to partake in the mission.

Bernard had his hands full once the crusade launched, as domestic disturbances began to erupt. Around this time, a French monk, whose name comes down to us as Rudolph, began to cause trouble by inciting mobs to persecute Jewish residents in the Rhineland. As was sadly all too often the case, Rudolph used the rationale that Christians should get rid of non-believers at home prior to waging war against non-believers abroad. But although some diabolical monks and some mobs of so-called Christians engaged in these nefarious acts, such things were never part of official church (as in the Catholic Church) policy.

And to Bernard's credit, he took immediate action as soon as he heard of the disturbance and personally intervened to stop the violence. He met with the riotous monk face to face, ordered him to stand down, and then sent him off to live in quiet exile in a monastery.

In the meantime, The Second Crusade began to take on multiple dimensions. Although the impetus for the Second Crusade was the loss of Edessa in the Holy Land, several side missions began to take shape. Soon after the call for another crusade was made, attention was drawn to the long struggle that had been waged to recover the Iberian Peninsula. The Iberian Peninsula, consisting of modern-day Spain and Portugal, had nearly been overrun by the Muslim forces.

Prior to the Islamic conquest, much of Iberia was under the rule of a European tribe known as the Visigoths. In 711, a group of Muslims known as the Berbers crossed the Strait of Gibraltar from North Africa and stormed into the peninsula. In a stunning defeat, the Visigoths were crushed, and almost all of the Iberian Peninsula became a part of Dar al Islam (The House of Islam.)

However, there were pockets of resistance, small enclaves where Christian kingdoms survived and would continue to do so for centuries. Right around the time of the Second Crusade, a leader of one of these Iberian enclaves, Afonso I Henriques of Portugal, was enlisting aid to recover the port city of Lisbon. With all of this talk of a crusade against the forces of Islam, Alfonso apparently figured it would be as good a time as any to ask for a helping hand.

And he received it. Crusaders from farther afield, such as the Flemings from Flanders, Belgium, who had planned to sail around the Iberian Peninsula, were redirected. Bernard of Clairvaux arranged for them to actually land on the peninsula instead of going around it just so they could hook up with Portuguese troops hellbent on recovering Lisbon. Although this event was viewed as a detour from the main mission, it would prove quite pivotal in the long run.

Islamic armies had been sweeping through the Near East, Middle East, and North Africa. They had been slowly encircling Christian Europe in what was essentially a pincer maneuver. As much as crusaders have been condemned through the years as bloodthirsty, religious zealots (some might even say idiots), if they had not stood up to this advance, one could easily envisage what would have been the result. It is likely that all of Byzantium, Greece, and the Balkans would have been overrun in the East, while Spain and France would have been entirely overtaken in the West. Both sides of the pincer would have then moved forward until the forces of Islam in the East linked up with the forces of Islam in the West, converging together right in the middle of Europe.

Bernard's decision during the Second Crusade to coordinate relief forces to land in Iberia was indeed pivotal in reversing this trend, continuing the long struggle known as the Reconquista.

We will cover the Reconquista itself in more depth a little later on in this book, but for now, just know the Second Crusade ultimately became tied together with this titanic struggle. And the redirection of troops from northern Europe to the frontlines of Iberia would be pivotal in not only reclaiming Lisbon for Portugal (Lisbon was successfully seized on October $24^{th}$, 1147) but also for helping to turn the tide against Islamic forces in Iberia.

Another side mission that took great importance during the Second Crusade was the forcible conversion/conquest of pagan Slavs in eastern Europe. This incident would set a precedent for other crusades against the pagan holdouts of eastern and northern Europe.

The main crusader force that had been dispatched for the main mission in the Middle East would largely meet with failure. The crusaders were harried all along the way by the Turks, who seemed to have foreseen their arrival ahead of time. Although there is no proof this was the case, it has long been suggested that the Byzantines forewarned the Turks. Byzantine politics in the region, with their constantly shifting alliances, were indeed complicated, but there is no hard evidence that any such advance notice was given to the Turks stationed in Anatolia.

It must be acknowledged that the Byzantines were often duplicitous and resentful to the Westerners, even when forced to seek out their aid. A lot of this bad blood can be traced directly back to the Great Schism of 1054 when the Catholic Church and the Eastern Orthodox Church excommunicated each other. Politics were also at play within the Byzantine Empire itself, as those with power wanted to make sure they held onto it.

At any rate, the main crusader force beat back several surprise ambushes before they finally made their way to Antioch. All of these ambushes took their toll on the crusaders. Upon arriving at Antioch on March 19th, 1148, King Louis VII led what remained of his crusaders into the city and held an audience with Raymond, the local ruler of Antioch. Almost immediately, there was a disagreement on how to proceed.

Raymond wanted the crusaders to aid him in his struggle against Aleppo, which he viewed as the "gateway" to retaking Edessa. However, King Louis VII wished to head to Jerusalem as soon as possible. The king apparently felt his own personal pilgrimage should take precedence over any further military maneuvers. There was even more drama by way of the king's wife, Eleanor. Eleanor had joined her husband, and it was noticed that she had taken a liking to Raymond. Soon, the court was swirling with gossip that something untoward might be in the works. Louis apparently believed the rumors and had his wife "arrested."

Louis took his wife with him, and he marched on to Jerusalem that April. Conrad and his fellow crusaders arrived shortly thereafter. In Jerusalem, the crusaders received a change of plans, as the plan was now to attack Damascus instead of Aleppo. The city-state of Damascus had been ruled by a string of various

Muslim potentates and had previously been an ally of the Kingdom of Jerusalem.

However, Damascus had recently switched sides, becoming friendly with Nur al-Din of Aleppo, and as such, it was now clearly a legitimate target of crusader aggression. The decision to attack Damascus would prove to be a great mistake, as it would come to derail the entire crusade.

The crusaders arrived at Damascus on July $4^{th}$, 1148. Initially, the crusaders had the advantage and plowed right through the outer defenses of the city. But once they broke through what has been described as "dense orchards" on the southern outskirts of the city, they found themselves in quite a bind. They had run out of water, and Nur al-Din and some rather heavy reinforcements were on the way to intercept them.

The crusaders were stranded out in the scorching heat and stuck between the walls of Damascus and a huge army with no water. Their position was most certainly not ideal. As such, the crusaders decided to make a hasty retreat. They were practically chased all the way back to the gates of Jerusalem. This utterly inglorious result marked the end of the Second Crusade.

# Chapter 5: The Third Crusade

*"We, however, place the love of God and his honor above our own and above the acquisition of many regions."*
-Richard I of England

As inglorious as much of the Second Crusade might have been, the Third Crusade would come to be known as one of the most heroic. It was also a crusade in which the stakes were much higher since the Third Crusade was launched in the aftermath of the fall of Jerusalem. Yes, Jerusalem had once again fallen, this time after the infamous Battle of Hattin in 1187. The Battle of Hattin was the end result of many years of Islamic attempts to take back Jerusalem.

In the aftermath of the Second Crusade, the Zengid dynasty was able to take control of a united Syria and then proceeded to take on the Fatimids of Egypt. The crusaders used to be rather fond of playing the Syrian faction against the Egyptian faction, and as it turns out, the real key to Islamic domination of the region was uniting Syria and Egypt. The man who managed to achieve this feat was an Islamic warlord and ingenious strategist named Saladin.

Saladin led this united Muslim force to take on the Kingdom of Jerusalem in the year 1187. The condition of the Crusader States also aided Saladin. The last great king of Jerusalem was Baldwin IV, the so-called "Leper King." Even though Baldwin IV was stricken with leprosy, he had proved himself to be an adept and able leader. He was also quite courageous, fearlessly leading armies on horseback, even though most in his condition probably would have been better off staying in bed.

Bandaged and essentially immune to pain due to his leprosy, Baldwin IV struck absolute terror in the hearts of his opponents. But eventually, the Leper King fell, and his nephew, Baldwin V, came to power. Baldwin V was just a child at the time, so the real power behind the throne was his mother, Sibylla, and her husband, Guy of Lusignan. Saladin rallied his mighty forces and struck out against weakened Jerusalem.

Saladin was an able strategist. He developed an ingenious plan that lured the main bulk of the crusader forces out of Jerusalem and into open combat, which, of course, was the very last thing the crusaders should have done. Out by the Horns of Hattin, the crusaders ended up becoming surrounded by enemy forces out in the middle of the scorching desert.

The place was (and still is) referred to as the "Horns of Hattin" because of its stark geographical features. There is an extinct volcano in the region, and the sides of it jut right out of the desert landscape, looking like the horns of some ancient beast stabbing the air. The crusaders fought bravely in the battle, but they ultimately were utterly annihilated.

Saladin then marched on Jerusalem. Although the defenders of the city held out as long as they could, they had to admit defeat. Jerusalem was lost to Christendom once again. Along with Jerusalem, Saladin seized a large chunk of other crusader territories, including the fortified coastal city of Acre. This was a tremendous blow to the crusaders. Therefore, the Third Crusade was called to recover these lost lands.

The Third Crusade is perhaps most notable because of the men who led it. Three of the leading figures of Europe from that age took part in and led this crusade: King Philip II of France, King Richard (otherwise known as Richard the Lionheart) of England, and Holy Roman Emperor Frederick Barbarossa. All but one of these men would make their way to the Holy Land.

Frederick Barbarossa, who was the Holy Roman emperor in addition to many other titles, such as the king of Italy, Germany, and Burgundy, perished on his way there in what was ostensibly a freak accident. He fell off his horse and was pitched into a river. Thanks to the heavy armor he wore, he drowned in the water. Barbarossa's premature death might have been somewhat decisive in the final outcome of the Third Crusade since it meant that most of the men Barbarossa led decided to return home once they learned their commander had died.

Only a small fraction of the troops Barbarossa led were determined enough to follow King Philip or King Richard. Thus, the crusader forces were greatly reduced once they reached the Holy Land. Had Barbarossa lived and led his full contingent, the crusaders would have been a much more formidable force.

It didn't help that Richard the Lionheart was distracted by a side adventure of his own. Prior to reaching the Holy Land, he made a pit stop in Cyprus, where he led his forces to victory and claimed the island.

Upon his arrival in Cyprus, Richard found the island under the control of a Greek despot named Isaac Komnenos, who had seized the territory from the Byzantine Empire in 1184. It serves as a great testament to just how weakened the Byzantines were. A rogue like Komnenos was able to snatch up such prime real estate since the Byzantines were unable to rally a sufficient enough force to take it back.

After Isaac Komnenos had seized both the passengers and cargo of a contingent of shipwrecked crusaders, Richard the Lionheart decided to take a detour and wage war on him. Isaac Komnenos apparently had bit off more than he could chew. When he saw the massive force that Richard had mustered against him, he quickly offered to surrender. He also agreed to pay money for all of the damages he had incurred upon the English subjects who had shipwrecked in Cyprus.

King Richard and those who chose to follow him left Cyprus and headed toward the mainland of the Levant. Richard and his men reached the gates of Acre in 1191, where they linked up with King Philip II of France and his troops.

Although Saladin had been victorious in the past, he apparently had bitten off a bit more than he could chew. He may have taken Acre, but he did not have enough troops left over to defend it.

The crusaders found the city sparsely defended and were able to easily conquer it.

After Acre was secured, King Philip quickly lost interest in the crusade, and he and most of his troops decided to ship off for home. However, Richard was not about to turn back as long as Jerusalem remained before him.

King Richard the Lionheart led the crusaders who were brave enough and willing to remain. Before heading for Jerusalem, Richard seized the strategic city of Jaffa, which lay on the road to the holy city. However, Saladin was not far behind and intercepted Richard's army some thirty miles north of the city. Saladin harried the rearguard and attempted to disrupt Richard's progress, but Richard, who was marching in sight of the coastline, was able to keep up a defensive position throughout the harassment. His troop formations did not break.

The final moment of truth came when a contingent of Knights Hospitaller defied Richard's orders to stay on the defensive. The Hospitallers suddenly charged at full speed into Saladin's army, slamming hard into Saladin's right flank. Richard realized he had to act and went ahead and ordered his forces to engage in an all-out attack. The two forces collided with each other near the town of Arsuf.

Richard's forces would prevail at the Battle of Arsuf, causing Saladin's army to retreat. This was a decisive win and cleared the crusaders' way to Jerusalem. Richard made his headquarters in Jaffa and prepared to lay siege to Jerusalem. He led his troops to the gates of the city in November 1191. However, once there, he soon realized that even if he overcame the Islamic defenders of Jerusalem, he would not have enough troops to hold the city. His success would be nothing since the city could very easily be retaken.

Richard realized how useless his position was and decided he might be better off negotiating a peace treaty with Saladin instead. Richard and Saladin had already been in talks through various intermediaries. Despite their ideological differences, the two had come to greatly respect each other as leaders. This alone made the idea of peace much more realistic. But before peace could happen, more fighting would occur.

In July 1192, Saladin attempted to retake Jaffa. Initially, Saladin was successful but faced a crisis when part of his army rebelled against him. Richard sent in reinforcements, and soon, Saladin's troops (those that were still under his control, at least) were pushed back. After this disastrous defeat, Saladin began to seriously consider entering into a peace treaty with Richard.

The final terms of peace were realized when the two men entered into a binding three-year truce, which began in September 1192. The truce ended the fighting; Saladin even guaranteed the free passage of Christians wishing to visit the holy sites of Jerusalem.

Many crusaders were saddened they had been unable to achieve the ultimate objective of taking Jerusalem, but they could at least be appeased that their struggle was not in vain. Saladin died in 1193, but the peace terms of the truce would still stand for some time. It would be right after the end of this three-year truce that the Fourth Crusade would be called.

# Chapter 6: The Fourth Crusade

*"European merchants supply the best weaponry, contributing to their own defeat."*

-*Saladin*

Richard the Lionheart managed to secure the entire coast of the Levant for Christendom, even though he did not actually retake Jerusalem. Even so, he had secured a respectable three-year truce with Saladin. But after those five years were up, the Fourth Crusade was called. Launched in 1202, the Fourth Crusade was engineered by Pope Innocent III. This crusade was largely just a mission to recoup the land that had been lost and that the Third Crusade had failed to recover. Jerusalem was perhaps the most important item on the crusade's agenda.

The Fourth Crusade, of course, sought to do what the Third Crusade could not: capture Jerusalem. But this crusade would have some serious problems from the very beginning. First of all, the crusaders would receive a pretty significant distraction when they became sidetracked fighting in the Christian city of Zara, located in modern-day Croatia.

Low on funds and morale, the crusaders then became embroiled in Byzantine politics when a claimant to the throne, Alexios Angelos, promised them they would have untold riches if they waged a campaign against the Byzantine Empire. Alexios's father had been the emperor, but Alexios's uncle deposed him.

Alexios sought to restore his father to the throne, even though he had been imprisoned and blinded.

But before the crusaders got involved in Zara or the Byzantine Empire, they had to address a problem of their own. They had come up short when paying the Republic of Venice for their services in ferrying the crusaders across the Mediterranean.

The crusaders were supposed to have more men, so the amount they had promised to pay just wasn't possible. Due to their lack of funds, the Venetian doge, Enrico Dandolo, suggested the crusaders could aid him in the capture of the city of Zara as part of the fulfillment of their debt. The doge's desire to take Zara was purely political since the city was occupied by fellow Christian believers. This meant the crusaders were breaking from their ideological convictions and attacking Christians rather than defending them.

It was hard for the crusaders to rationalize this attack as other than a means of making a little money to pay off their debts. This event greatly corrupted the morale of the crusaders, who were now not fighting for a larger-than-life cause but fighting for mere material gain. They had essentially become little more than mercenaries.

The crusaders were successful in seizing Zara for the doge, but as soon as the pope heard about it, he had them all excommunicated. (He would later lift the excommunication but kept the excommunication of the Venetians intact because he believed they were to blame.) Rather than boldly storming into the Holy Land for the cause of Christendom, the crusaders had become a large body of excommunicated heretics.

However, it is important to note that although the leaders of the Fourth Crusade realized they had been excommunicated, the average soldier did not. The excommunication was carefully concealed from the rank-and-file members of the crusader forces, as the leaders knew the men would leave if they found out.

In January 1203, these crestfallen crusaders were contacted by a former Byzantine prince named Alexios Angelos. Alexios sought to suck the crusaders into Byzantine politics, pleading for them to restore his deposed father, Isaac II Angelos, as emperor. It was then that a hare-brained scheme was concocted between the

Venetians and the leaders of the crusaders to restore the Byzantine Angelos line to the throne and then use the money from the Byzantine treasury to finance the journey to Jerusalem.

The plans for this plot simmered for several months before the crusaders finally reached the gates of the great Byzantine capital, Constantinople, that June. The battle initially commenced on the outskirts of Constantinople in the suburban areas of Chrysopolis and Chalcedon. During this engagement, the crusaders were greatly outnumbered but charged the Byzantines on horseback. Surprisingly and against the odds, the crusaders managed to defeat the Byzantines' larger force.

This victory no doubt buoyed their spirits. Riding high on this victory, the crusader forces made use of naval craft to make their way over the Bosporus. Interestingly enough, the crusader fleet soon sailed within sight of Constantinople with the Byzantine prince who had asked for help standing on the deck. To the bewilderment of the crusaders, the citizens of Constantinople did not let out a deafening cry of support. They instead gathered on the walls to jeer and mock the unwanted Byzantine prince. Even though Alexios's uncle was a usurper, the people liked him. Nevertheless, the crusaders were hellbent on installing the proper heir to the Byzantine throne, whether the Byzantines liked it or not.

The Byzantines went on the offensive and unleashed an army of around 8,500 troops. Alexios III, the usurper, led them right through Constantinople's Gate of St. Romanus. The Byzantine army dwarfed the crusader force, which comprised around 3,500 warriors. However, the Byzantines had a problem. For whatever reason, Emperor Alexios III was just not cut out for fighting. He became terribly discouraged and suddenly ordered his troops to retreat. He should have been able to use his mighty force to push back the invaders but instead ended up humiliating himself and his subjects with an unnecessary withdrawal.

In fact, Alexios III was so humiliated that he fled his own kingdom later that night. Demonstrating just how quickly the sands of fate could shift for a Byzantine ruler, Alexios III was deposed, and Isaac II was put back on the throne.

However, there was a problem. Isaac had been blinded to ensure he could not rule. The crusaders insisted that Prince Alexios step up to rule alongside him. Plus, what better way to ensure Alexios followed through on his promise of payment than by making him co-emperor? Prince Alexios became Alexios IV.

And then came the other problem. There just wasn't enough money in the treasury to fully pay what Alexios had promised the crusaders. It was certainly a rough spot to be in; he didn't want to upset the people he ruled too much by draining the treasury and raising taxes, but he also didn't want to upset the crusaders, who could potentially sack the city and wreak havoc because they weren't paid.

Alexios was able to come up with half the money by taking goods from the churches and selling off lands. But the crusaders weren't satisfied with half. And the people weren't satisfied with Alexios's rule. His father also resented sharing the throne with him.

In 1203, violence broke out between the crusaders and the people of the city. Alexios refused to give in to the crusaders' demands, but even this outspokenness against the crusaders failed to gain him favor with the people. In January 1204, a popular uprising dethroned Alexios. He and his father were imprisoned and killed (it is believed Isaac might have died of old age).

Alexios IV's death gave the crusaders the justification to satisfied go on the offensive. In April 1204, days after Alexios was murdered, the crusaders ruthlessly occupied the city and drained it of much of its wealth. The Byzantines eventually regrouped around their old capital, Nicaea.

The Byzantines established a strong resistance, and in 1261, under Byzantine Emperor Michael VIII Palaeologus, the crusaders were finally driven out. Even so, the Byzantine Empire would never quite recover from the desolation that had been wrought by the Fourth Crusade. The pope condemned the action, but the damage was done. Orthodox Christians were shocked at what the crusaders had done, and it seemed as if the rift between the two churches would never be patched now (although it is unlikely it would have been patched even if this incident hadn't occurred).

It is ironic that the Fourth Crusade, which began with the same religious fervor and anticipation as the First, Second, and Third crusades, ended without any of the crusaders so much as stepping foot in the Holy Land.

# Chapter 7: The Fifth and Sixth Crusades

*"In order to avoid contention, never contradict anyone, except in case of sin or some danger to a neighbor; and when necessary to contradict others, and to oppose your opinion to theirs, do it with so much mildness and tact, as not to appear to do violence to their mind, for nothing is ever gained by taking up things with excessive warmth and hastiness."*

*-King Louis IX*

The Fifth Crusade was initially called by Pope Innocent III at the Fourth Lateran Council in 1215. You might recognize the name; it was the same pope who called for the Fourth Crusade, which had ended in the disastrous seizure of Constantinople and the excommunication of the crusader force (although by the time of the Fourth Lateran Council, he had revoked the excommunication). Pope Innocent was appalled at what these crusaders had done and actively sought to make amends by calling for yet another crusade.

But in the aftermath of his abrupt passing in 1216, the commencement of this crusade was inherited by the next pope, Honorius III. The Fifth Crusade, predictably enough, had the same intention as the previous two crusades: the recovery of Jerusalem. But even though Jerusalem was the goal, a slight detour was yet again in the works. It had been suggested that perhaps it would be easier to drive through the soft underbelly of Egypt to get there. Interestingly enough, it was none other than Richard the Lionheart who first suggested this all the way back in the Third Crusade. Few agreed with his strategy back then, but views on this idea had changed by the time of the Fifth Crusade.

So, an all-out assault was launched on the Ayyubid-controlled Egyptian territory of Damietta. On May 27$^{th}$, 1218, the crusaders landed in Damietta, Egypt. The crusaders then laid siege to the city on June 23$^{rd}$ of the same year. They made use of some eighty ships and a whole host of impressive siege equipment. Some of the siege engines had "revolving ladders" and were covered in flame-resistant furs in case the defenders used Greek fire. This sticky, flammable substance was basically an ancient version of napalm.

The fact the crusaders had planned for such contingencies shows they were not taking this adventure lightly. Even so, the city was heavily fortified, and this first incursion was easily repulsed. The crusaders were relentless and proceeded to attack the city once again. On August 24$^{th}$, the main tower of the city was seized, and the chains stretched across the Nile to block the intruders were severed.

These developments proved to be too much for the leader of the city, Sultan al-Adil, who perished right after he heard the news of what had happened (it is unknown how he died). He was immediately succeeded by his son and heir, al-Kamil, who made sure that he shored up what remained of the defenses. These measures included wrecking ships in the Nile to create a defensive barrier.

The sultan's ingenious move put off further offensives for some time. The crusaders were forced to wait it out.

In the meantime, relief forces arrived, with the papal legate, Pelagius Galvani, in its train. Pope Innocent III desired for the Roman Catholic Church to take on a more direct role in this crusade in light of the failures of the Fourth Crusade, which had infamously resulted in the whole group getting excommunicated. It was reasoned that if a papal authority led the crusade, the crusaders would stay on track to achieve their actual objectives.

The influx of French soldiers that the legate brought with him did much to bolster the strength of the crusaders. But throughout much of 1219, the two sides were locked in a bloody quagmire of fighting.

It wasn't until November of that year that the crusaders finally managed to prevail and seize the city. But even though the city was taken, the sultan was not defeated; he simply moved his army farther south.

In the end, the crusader victory at Damietta proved to be a costly one and was not really worth the effort. The crusaders found themselves in control of a city surrounded by enemies. They did not have the people or resources to adequately defend Damietta. The Fifth Crusade ultimately came to a close in 1221 by way of a truce. The truce was basically the negotiated surrender of Damietta, in which the defenders were allowed to depart in peace.

Although the Fifth Crusade seemed to accomplish very little, it had its interesting moments, including when a famous monk, Saint Francis of Assisi, arrived in Egypt in 1219 in the midst of the fighting to preach the Gospel to crusaders and Muslims. In fact, it has even been said that he gained an audience with the sultan himself. Not much is known of what was said (some postulate that Francis tried to convert the sultan to Catholicism), but regardless of what was discussed, the sultan was quite intrigued by the boldness of the Christian monk who had come to visit him. It is also theorized that Saint Francis of Assisi perhaps paved the way for a lasting truce between the two warring parties.

The Sixth Crusade was a direct consequence of the failures of the Fifth Crusade. Many historians do not even recognize the Sixth Crusade, as it is sometimes simply referred to as the Crusade of Frederick II since it was largely led and engineered by German Holy Roman Emperor Frederick. Frederick II was largely making up for the fact that he did not take part in the Fifth Crusade.

It was not because he didn't want to fight in the Fifth Crusade. Frederick had pledged to take part but ended up being too late to do so. So, the Sixth Crusade could be seen as the Holy Roman emperor's effort to make amends. Even so, this so-called crusade had hardly any fighting to speak of and largely depended on the political machinations of Frederick II.

Holy Roman Emperor Frederick II successfully negotiated a treaty with al-Kamil that secured peace and granted Christians the control of Jerusalem for a period of ten years as long as the city remained unfortified and the previously demolished walls were not rebuilt. There was also the stipulation that Al-Aqsa Mosque, which the Templars had famously converted into their so-called "Temple of Solomon" headquarters, would remain exclusively under Muslim control.

The terms were a very small price to pay to have Jerusalem back under Christian control. The notion that Jerusalem could be taken without bloodshed was unheard of, yet Fredrick managed to do it.

Even so, his effort was largely unappreciated by Christians and Muslims at the time. In the zero-sum ideological game that was being played, both sides viewed such active cooperation with the supposed enemy as tantamount to treason. Although the peaceful use of Jerusalem by all parties was the result, both sides felt that such a settlement was absurd. And predictably enough, after the ten-year truce was over, the fighting would begin once again.

# Chapter 8: The Barons' Crusade

*"A crusade is, simply put, something that's bigger than you are. It's a cause with an impact that reaches beyond your personal wants and needs."*

-Arthur L. Williams, Jr.

After the Fifth and Sixth Crusades, the numbering of the Crusades gets much harder to keep up with. At this point in history, they branch off into side crusades that had many different names and many different objectives. Among them was the so-called "Barons' Crusade." This particular effort was led by Theobald I (sometimes also known as Thibaut), who was the count of Champagne and the king of Navarre.

And as you might have guessed, the leading lights of the Barons' Crusade were all barons or nobles of some kind or other. It was a veritable who's who of medieval nobility: Hugh IV, Duke of Burgundy; Amaury I of Montfort (son of the famous Simon de Montfort, who also took part); and Richard of Cornwall, just to name a few.

Theobald's army consisted of around 1,500 knights and many infantry units. He led all of them to the Levant. Theobald's troops made their way to the gates of Acre on September 1$^{st}$, 1239. Here, these nobles were met by homegrown nobles, and the next several weeks would be wasted with frivolous pleasantries.

Nevertheless, the Barons' Crusade would ultimately prove to be much more successful than many that had come before it and any that came after. In November, Theobald led his troops out of Acre and marched to Ascalon, which had been a crusader stronghold since 1153. They erected a fortified castle once they arrived.

However, during the march, one of the nobles, Peter I, Duke of Brittany, broke away from the main group and conducted a punitive raid on a passing Muslim caravan. This was a fairly dreadful act on the part of the crusaders, as the caravan drivers were slaughtered and their goods seized. It was not as much an act of war as it was blatant murder and theft. Nevertheless, the crusader forces were bolstered by the goods that had been taken.

After the crusaders reached Gaza, another faction announced its intention to conduct a raid. This time around, Theobald directly ordered them to stand down. But even after being given direct orders to cease and desist by Theobald and the leaders of the monastic knights who were with them, the men blatantly defied the commands given to them and launched their raid regardless. They headed south toward Gaza, but this time around, the raiders were not successful. Rather than meeting up with a caravan of merchants, they were waylaid by a fully equipped army. The would-be raiders were subsequently annihilated.

The ten-year truce that had given Christians control of Jerusalem was up, and the Muslim forces understandably, considering the sudden onslaught of violence waged against them, retook control of the city. At this point, it must have seemed that yet another crusade was being met with disaster, even if it wasn't an official crusade. But the winds of fate would soon change in the crusaders' favor, as the local Islamic powers began to fight amongst each other.

Sultan al-Kamil had passed away, and the various Ayyubid factions were in chaos while they searched for a successor. The most likely choices were the sultan's sons, al-Adil II and as-Salih Ayuub. But there were also those who backed al-Kamil's brother, as-Salih Ismail, as well as Ismail's son, an-Nasir Dawud. An-Nasir Dawud would momentarily seize control of Jerusalem after the end of the ten-year truce that had been orchestrated by Frederick II.

However, Count Theobald, who was not one to be outdone, indicated that he was ready to try his hand at diplomacy. He entered into negotiations with Sultan an-Nasir Dawud of Damascus and sought to gain an alliance against their mutual enemies in Egypt on the condition that Jerusalem, as well as Sidon, Tiberias, Galilee, and southern Palestine, were returned to the crusaders.

With the sultan of Damascus in his back pocket, Theobald led an army against the Egyptians. The Egyptians ended up standing down at Jaffa. Since Theobald had already hammered out the terms of the treaty with the sultan of Damascus, he saw no reason to take Jaffa. Instead, Theobald secured the terms of his treaty. This meant that Jerusalem was once again in Christian control.

Figuring that his work was done, Theobald then set sail for home in the fall of 1240. Further reinforcements from England would arrive that October when Richard of Cornwall landed in the Holy Land with a significant force. These reinforcements were used to shore up the crusaders' defensive positions.

Even so, it was a rather tenuous grip. Even though Jerusalem was temporarily reclaimed, it would be lost once again in 1244 when a powerful Islamic army led by the Khwarazmians—a Turkish group of warriors fighting for the Egyptians—wrested Jerusalem from the crusaders.

The Khwarazmians, who originated from central Asia, had been displaced by the Mongol invasions that were first sparked by the warlord Genghis Khan. They had since relocated to regions in Iraq and Syria, where they solidified their strength prior to invading the crusader-held territories in and around Jerusalem.

There is an interesting account of what life was like in the city just prior to the Khwarazmian conquest of it. The report comes from an Islamic scholar named Ibn Wasil, who arrived from Cairo to visit the city.

Although Muslims were still granted free access to Jerusalem under Christian occupation, Ibn Wasil was aghast at what he saw. He spoke of his disgust at seeing Christian priests openly preaching and praying inside the Muslim holy site called Dome of the Rock. He was also outraged to see the sacred Al-Aqsa Mosque (which the Knights Templar had previously used as their own headquarters) "decorated with bells." Ibn Wasil had long been critical of Christian control of the city ever since Frederick II diplomatically secured the arrangement back in 1229.

In the summer of 1244, Ibn felt it was high time that someone did something about the Christians controlling Jerusalem. Just a few months later, his prayers were answered. Al-Kamil's son, al-Salih Ayuub, secured a strategic partnership with the newcomers on the scene, the Khwarazmians. On July 11th, 1244, they rolled right into Jerusalem. Just as the Khwarazmians had been displaced by the Mongols, they returned the favor by displacing the Christians of Jerusalem.

The city was quite easy to invade since the city walls had never been rebuilt. And once inside, the Khwarazmians were absolutely ruthless. They cut off the heads of priests and worshipers. They desecrated the Church of the Holy Sepulchre and raided the tombs of crusader kings (save the Leper King, which was left alone).

The military orders of the Knights Templars, Knights Hospitallers, Teutonic Knights, and Leper Knights tried their best to protect civilians. They attempted to establish a corridor through which the people could be led to safety, but the task proved far too difficult against such an onslaught.

An account of the event from a Knight Hospitaller survived. Gerald of Newcastle was one of the lucky ones who lived to tell the tale. As Gerald describes it, "The enemy surrounding them on all sides, attacked them with swords, arrows, stones and other weapons, slew and cut [to] pieces around seven thousand men and women and caused such a massacre that the blood of those of the faith ran down the sides of the mountains like water."

Even so, this was not the end of the struggle against the Khwarazmians. The Christians were not going to allow the city to be taken without a fight. The crusaders rallied their forces and secured auxiliary Muslim troops from the sultan of Damascus, with whom they were allied. This led to a confrontation on October 17th between the crusader and Damascene troops and a contingent of Khwarazmian and Egyptian warriors near Gaza.

Although the town today is known by its Arabic name al-Hiribya, the crusaders knew it as La Forbie. So, the ensuing apocalyptic battle that took place here would be known as the infamous Battle of La Forbie. The crusader and Damascene forces were outnumbered, but they fought so ferociously that it was not at all clear who might come out on top.

However, the fate of the crusaders was sealed when their Damascene allies ultimately became spooked and fled the battle. No matter how hard the crusaders fought, the situation was now utterly impossible. The crusaders' tattered army, which was entirely dwarfed by their opponents, was easily crushed. All hope for a victorious outcome in the Barons' Crusade was dashed.

# Chapter 9: Louis IX's and Prince Edward's Crusades

*"In prosperity, give thanks to God with humility and fear lest by pride you abuse God's benefits and so offend him."*

-*King Louis IX*

In December 1244, the very same year that Jerusalem was lost to the Khwarazmians, the king of France, Louis IX, lay on what was believed to be his deathbed. He had been suffering for some time from a bad case of dysentery. Reduced to skin and bones by the chronic illness, he was so weak that he was barely breathing. Yet, when those in attendance felt that all was lost and were on the verge of giving him up for dead, Kind Louis made what seemed to be a miraculous recovery.

His eyes suddenly opened wide. He gasped and immediately requested that he be brought his Crusader's cross. King Louis fully believed that he had just been brought back from the brink of death to call for a crusade to reclaim Jerusalem. King Louis IX was ready to lead the latest march to the Holy Land. And he would choose a familiar route to get there.

Louis was unconcerned about the failure of the Fifth Crusade, which ran aground in Damietta, Egypt, as he called for the crusaders to reach Jerusalem again by driving through Egypt. Despite the Barons' Crusade's previous failure, going through

Egypt made some strategic sense. The sultan that was behind the Khwarazmian invasion of Jerusalem in 1244, al-Salih, was based out of Egypt. It only made sense that the crusaders would want to take the fight directly to the figure perceived as being their archnemesis at the time.

The sultan turned on his Khwarazmian allies almost as soon as they won the city of Jerusalem for him. Al-Salih no longer had any use for the Khwarazmians, so he rallied his own forces and drove them from the city. If it had been possible, the cleverest move the crusaders could have made at that point would have been to somehow link up with the Khwarazmians.

After all, the Khwarazmians were probably more than ready to seek vengeance against the sultan. An alliance between the crusaders and Khwarazmians would have been a classic case of "an enemy of my enemy is my friend," in which two adversaries temporarily forget their differences to team up against a mutual foe. It would have been interesting to see what the end results of such an unlikely partnership would have been.

However, that is not how history played itself out. The crusaders had no such strategic alliance and instead stormed the beaches (in their own medieval version of D-Day) in June 1249 and took on the enemy by themselves. The sultan and his troops were waiting for them, with horns blaring and drums pounding. If they thought this display would frighten the Christian trespassers, they were mistaken.

King Louis IX was a man of conviction after his near-death experience. And he fearlessly disembarked from his ship as soon as land was in sight, leading his troops to charge the enemy head-on. Accompanying them was Walter of Brienne, who had only recently been ransomed after he was made a prisoner of war in the aftermath of the disastrous Battle of La Forbie.

The sultan had a formidable army that was led by an equally formidable general, Fakhr al-Din. As such, it's a bit surprising that as soon as the crusaders charged, Fakhr al-Din ordered his troops to withdraw instead of crushing the invaders on the shoreline. Even stranger, he ordered Damietta to be evacuated. The crusaders ended up marching into an empty city. For many, it must have seemed as if a divine hand was at work, but their

Egyptian opponents had their own reasons for taking these measures.

Fakhr al-Din was a student of history, and he knew how difficult it was for the crusaders to hold the city during the Fifth Crusade. As such, he figured simply letting them have it (and, as a consequence, letting them deal with all of the burdens of upkeep and defense that came with it) would harm them more than it would do them any good.

The Egyptian general regrouped his forces farther up the Nile at the heavily fortified site of al-Mansurah. He patiently waited for the crusaders to meet their doom at this spot. They would either have to march up the Nile to do battle with the Egyptians, which put them at a decided disadvantage, or waste away in Damietta. Each of these was a bad choice; which one they would make was up to them.

In November 1249, the crusader forces determined the Nile had receded enough to continue their invasion farther up the river. This could have been a fortuitous time for them since it was right around this period that Sultan al-Salih abruptly passed away. His general, Fakhr al-Din, wisely kept his death a complete secret as he secured his own grip on power.

Fakhr al-Din also made sure he organized his army into a formidable fighting machine. At the head of his army was a special contingent of warriors known as Bahriyya, which is Arabic for "of the river." This group, which is often likened to an Islamic version of the Knights Templar, was fierce, fearless, and fully dedicated to the cause. This tremendous force waited for the crusaders to arrive.

In December—Christmas Day no less—King Louis IX's forces finally made their way to al-Mansurah, arriving at the opposite side of the Tanis River, where they found themselves facing their opponents. Although separated by water, the two sides began skirmishing. King Louis IX's engineers began vigorously working on pontoon bridges, with which it was hoped that a crossing could be made.

In February 1250, the crusader camp was approached by a local Bedouin man, who convinced them that he could lead them to a narrow portion of the river that could be crossed by horse. He promised to divulge this information for the small price of "five hundred bezants." The crusaders figured this was as good an opportunity as any and took him up on the offer. They were able to cross the river but were easily spotted by a reconnaissance force while doing so.

The reconnaissance force wheeled around and rushed off to inform Fakhr al-Din of the news. The crusaders should have allowed their forces to fully cross and consolidate themselves so they would be better prepared for a pitched battle when it arrived. By doing so, they could have taken advantage of the time lag, as the reconnaissance team had to ride to inform Fakhr.

But instead, the crusaders who had crossed immediately charged at the reconnaissance troops, apparently hoping to annihilate them before they reached Fakhr. They ended up chasing the group all the way to the streets of al-Mansurah. If Fakhr didn't know of their arrival before then, he most certainly would have known by that point. As the crusaders crashed through the city, they very loudly announced their presence.

So, rather than picking the most optimal locale to engage the enemy, the crusaders became bogged down in violent and bloody street fighting. And as the enemy regrouped and reinforced their numbers, the crusaders were easily swarmed in the unfamiliar urban terrain. Hit from all sides, the crusader troops were hacked apart. Hundreds of knights were killed, including some 280 Knights Templar, who seemed to take the brunt of the assault.

Needless to say, the crusaders were pushed back. By April, it seemed that all hope of recovery was lost. An all-out retreat was ordered on April 5th, with the crusaders fleeing down the Nile as they were hacked and hammered by the enemy the whole way. Even worse, in the chaotic melee, King Louis IX himself was captured. His capture brought true meaning to the phrase "a king's ransom," as those holding King Louis demanded a huge amount of money to secure his freedom.

For those who had survived, it was relayed to them that the king would not be released unless 800,000 gold bezants were delivered to the sultan's camp. The king's men did not have that much money on them, but they knew who did: the Knights Templar. The Templars had long served as a kind of banking institution and had enormous wealth. However, the Templars could not just hand over such a huge amount since the money they guarded was deposited by others.

The surviving marshal of the order, Renaud de Vichiers, sympathized with the king of France and wanted him released as much as anyone else. As such, he came up with a crafty ploy to do so without having to break any of his personal vows in the process.

As the king's French troops stood by, Renaud loudly proclaimed that he could not possibly lend any money and that if the French happened to take their money by force, then the Templars would be forced to take reparations upon their return to the crusader stronghold of Acre. The French quickly understood the game the Templar marshal was playing. Although Renaud was bound by oath to safeguard the funds, he would not be held responsible if the French seized it by force.

As such, a small contingent of French troops stormed the Templars' galley and forcibly seized enough money to free their king. While this happened, the Knights Templar stood idly by; they did not break any oath, but they also did not put up any resistance either. As a result of these machinations, King Louis was freed. On May 13$^{th}$, 1250, he made his way to Acre.

He spent the next few years in that city doing his best to ensure that as many Christian prisoners of war from the Egyptian debacle were freed as possible. For these good works, King Louis IX would later be canonized as a saint. Additionally, many geographical regions would be named after this king and saint (for instance, Saint Louis, Missouri, and the Saint Louis River, both of which are in the US).

Despite this posthumous acclaim, Louis would return home in 1254, greatly disappointed that his mission ended in what he could only see as an abject failure. However, he would try again. Several years later, in 1270, he picked up a powerful ally, Prince Edward of England (the future King Edward I of England). Prince Edward's father, King Henry III, was far too old for such an adventure, but his energetic son was more than up for the challenge.

As soon as all of the papal blessings and financial arrangements were made, Edward was ready to disembark for the Holy Land.

But King Louis, who was again leading the charge, once again had his sights set on North Africa instead. This time, he wanted to seize the Muslim-controlled city of Tunis and make it his forward base of operations. It was believed that Tunis could be used as a Mediterranean supply depot and a launching point for an overland march through Egypt and then on into the Holy Land.

But as fate would have it, King Louis would perish that August while Prince Edward was en route. After Louis's death, a truce was negotiated with the emir of Tunis. Ironically enough, by the time Edward landed, he was informed that the crusade was over. Unsure of what else to do, Edward and his troops sailed from Tunis and landed in Sicily, where they spent the winter. They then headed to that last great bastion of the Crusader States in the Levant: Acre.

Prince Edward arrived at the city of Acre on May 9th, 1271. The situation was a fairly desperate one for the crusaders, as they struggled to hang onto their remaining toehold in the Holy Land. In fact, just prior to Edward's landing, the once-mighty French castle, which had long stood just outside of Acre, known as Krak des Chevaliers, had just been taken by Islamic forces.

The crusaders' main antagonist at this time was a local sultan named al-Malik al-Zahir Baibars (also spelled Baybars). Shortly after Edward's arrival, the sultan rode to the gates of Acre with a large force, not to fight but to openly mock and taunt the crusaders holed up inside the city. Although Prince Edward came with a small army that numbered only in the hundreds, his arrival boosted morale. However, he and his troops would not be enough to turn the tide. Prince Edward quickly realized that open combat would spell disaster. Nevertheless, he wanted to do what he could to strike out against the antagonists of Christendom, so he began to conduct hit-and-run raids. However, these attacks were not carried out against soldiers; they were being conducted against civilian targets, making them little more than terrorist-styled attacks. These attacks were undoubtedly cowardly, as the only real reason Edward targeted civilians was that they were much easier to subdue.

Deep down, Edward must have known that such acts were certainly not befitting of a Christian prince of his stature. Yet, it seemed that such petty, punitive actions were all that he was capable of carrying out. But he soon had bigger fish to fry. He began to engineer an outright collaboration with one of Islam's greatest foes: the Mongols. Edward sent an envoy to the Mongol warlord Abaqa Khan and persuaded the Mongols to attack the city of Aleppo, located in modern-day Syria. This would put the Mongol forces just northeast of Acre.

The plan was to use the Mongol attack on Aleppo as a distraction. So, when the Mongols attacked, the crusaders could march right up to an undefended Jerusalem. But the crusaders first had to take out an important fortress called Qaqun, which stood as a watchtower between Acre and Jerusalem.

Edward and his troops, along with a group of Knights Hospitaller and Knights Templar, marched on the fortress. The group was only able to reach the very edge of the citadel before they were waylaid by enemy forces. Their opponents proved too formidable, and they had to retreat. This humiliating retreat led to nothing but mockery from Sultan Baibars.

It has been said that the sultan proclaimed, "If so many men cannot take a house [the fortress of Qaqun], it seems unlikely that they will conquer the kingdom of Jerusalem." Even so, Edward still attempted to come up with a plan for a renewed assault. But after he was very nearly killed by one of Baibars's infamous assassins, he finally admitted defeat and began his long trek back to England.

However, he did not leave before gaining Baibars's pledge to agree to a ten-year truce. Baibars would perish five years later. Some have theorized that he was poisoned by one of his own assassins. At any rate, the last remnants of the Crusader States would soon be in jeopardy once again.

# Chapter 10: The Fall of the Crusader States

*"Every war is its own excuse. That's why they're all surrounded with ideals. That's why they're all crusades."*

-Karl Shapiro

The year 1291 would be an infamous one, for this would be the year that the final toehold of the Crusader States in the Holy Land would be lost. The successor of Baibars—Sultan al-Ashraf Khalil—would deal the crusaders their final blow.

By 1291, much of Europe had put the Crusades on the back burner. It just was not a priority for most of the European leaders at the time. With no large crusader force from Europe forthcoming, the main defenders of the city of Acre were the resident military orders: the Templars, Hospitallers, and Teutonic Knights. There were even a handful of Leper Knights from the Order of Saint Lazarus. All of these knights were willing to give their lives for the city of Acre and its forty thousand residents. Many of them ultimately did.

The new sultan began to plan what would be the final assault on the city in March 1291. The sultan's forces surrounded Acre and made their camp right outside the city's walls. They began their assault on April 5th but not before providing an opportunity for those inside to surrender. It had long been a part of Islamic tradition to allow a city's inhabitants a chance to voluntarily submit to Islam.

This does not mean the residents had to convert. Rather, the residents had to accept the authority of Islam. Christians would remain unharmed as long as they paid the jizya (a religious tax) and submitted to the terms that went with being a second-class citizen. However, the defenders of Acre had not spent their whole lives struggling to maintain their hold on the Holy Land just to give up now.

There was also no real guarantee that their conquerors would hold up their part of the bargain. Although these were the general rules of Islamic warfare, there was so much hatred and antagonism between the two camps by this point that it would have been hard to say whether such terms would have been held up even if the crusaders laid down their arms and agreed to them. The chivalrous days of Richard the Lionheart and Saladin were long gone and had been replaced by two hundred or so years of endless animosity.

The crusaders felt they had only one option—to fight on. So, when they received word the sultan was willing to discuss the terms of their surrender, the crusaders answered by hurling arrows, stones, and garbage at the sultan's messengers.

The crusaders then fortified their defenses and prepared for the inevitable assault. They also attempted to sabotage the Muslims. In the middle of the night, a group of knights from the Order of Saint Lazarus actually snuck out of Acre and attempted to destroy the sultan's siege engines. If they had been successful, this would have significantly diminished the sultan's ability to wage war. However, these leper-stricken knights ultimately failed in their efforts, as their horses got tripped up in the tent rope lines that crisscrossed all over the sultan's camp.

The resulting tumult brought the enemy down upon the Leper Knights, and they were quickly dispatched. Just a few weeks later, on May 14$^{th}$, the sultan led his final assault on Acre. His siege engines tore through the city walls as planned, and his troops poured into the city. Hospitallers, Templars, Teutonic Knights, and Leper Knights all engaged the enemy and fought with everything they had. The only real reinforcements were a handful of knights sent from England. But this was just a drop in the bucket, and their opponents' larger numbers would overwhelm them soon enough.

The small group of tattered knights who survived made their way to the Templar fortress known as the "Templar House." They safeguarded civilians who ran to the fortress for refuge. The sultan initially promised safe passage for the civilians who remained, promising to escort them to a nearby port with his own men so that they could be evacuated from the city. Many had already attempted to make their way to the port only to be trodden by the hooves of the invaders' horses.

The chaotic conditions were quite dangerous. For example, the patriarch of Jerusalem, Nicolas of Hanapes, lost his life simply slipping off a boat and perishing in the waters. But feeling as if this was the only chance they had to shepherd the remaining civilians out of Acre, the Templars agreed to the proposition. But after they opened the gates to the citadel and their Muslim escorts entered the Templar House, it is said they began mistreating the women and children.

Some accounts dispute the notion that the women and children were mistreated or harassed, but something seems to have provoked the Templars, as it seems unlikely they would attack for no reason after giving their word. For whatever reason, the enraged marshal, Peter de Sevrey, decided to go back on the agreement, slamming the gates shut and locking a few hundred enemy combatants inside. The surviving Templars, Hospitallers, Teutons, and Leper Knights tore into their enemies, making short work of them.

The sultan was very weary of the prolonged struggle and wished to put an end to it. He ordered his engineers to plant explosives around the foundation of the Templar House.

The explosives managed to tear through the walls of the compound. The sultan's forces then stormed into the building. But as soon as they did, the whole building collapsed down upon them. Everyone inside was killed when the roof caved in. The crusaders and those under their charge had perished. This was the end of the crusader stronghold of Acre, and with its fall came an end to the Crusader States.

# Part Two: Other Crusades

# Chapter 11: The Northern Crusades

*"Any crusade requires optimism and the ambition to aim high."*
*-Paul Allen*

The Northern Crusades were actually a series of expeditions against the pagan holdouts in northeastern Europe. The Northern Crusades relied upon the precedent of battling pagans that had been established during the Wendish Crusade, as well as the efforts of Holy Roman Emperor Charlemagne the Great, who had waged war on the pagans of Saxony (modern-day Denmark). The actual starting point of what has been lumped together as the Northern Crusades is believed to be when Pope Celestine III called for action in 1195.

The call to arms was issued, and the Livonian Knights, or Brothers of the Sword, found themselves knee-deep in warfare with the remnants of European paganism in the early 1200s. Livonia made up much of the eastern shores of the Baltic Sea in northeastern Europe, which today makes up the modern-day nations of Latvia, Lithuania, and Estonia. This region became ground zero for Christian missionaries wishing to convert the local pagans. It also saw increased settlement by western (predominantly German-speaking) European peoples.

As the inevitable conflict between Christians and pagans escalated, it was determined that the region would benefit from a permanent military order entrusted with the protection of Christians and the active conversion of pagans. Albert, Bishop of Riga, founded the Livonian Order in 1202. Shortly thereafter, the Livonian Knights were locked into increasingly hostile combat with (predominantly Lithuanian) pagan warriors.

The order itself had many early victories but was nearly annihilated in 1236 during the Battle of Saule, in which the Lithuanians rallied and unleashed a ferocious onslaught upon them. Many of their number, including their grand master, were killed in battle. After this incident, the remnants of the Livonian Knights were subsequently absorbed into the Teutonic Knights. The merger appears to have been completed by 1237.

The Teutonic Knights have an interesting history that should be addressed in some greater depth. The order began its existence in the Holy Land as the guardians of the Hospital of Saint Mary. After the initial loss of Jerusalem in 1187, they shifted focus to Acre. But after the fall of Acre, they were forced to shift gears once again. And once the Holy Land had been lost completely, the vast majority of Teutonic Knights ended up redeploying to Livonia.

The pope decreed that a new crusade against the pagans of Livonia was in the works and even declared that Livonia was the "land of the Mother of God." Such things sound a bit bizarre, considering the fact the northeastern European lands of the Baltic are fairly far away from the Middle East, but in those days, the pope's words were powerful. And if he declared it to be so, it must be. Additionally, the pope's words added to the mystique and attraction of crusading and potentially dying in an effort to subdue pagan lands.

But the Teutonic Knights would not only butt heads with the pagans. They also got into the bad graces of the Russian Orthodox Christians. The Russians were part of the Christian family, but the family had broken apart back in 1054, with Eastern Orthodoxy on one side and the Catholic Church on the other. The animosity over their religious differences and perhaps the fear that the Eastern Orthodox members would convert the Livonian pagans before the Catholics had the chance would lead to an armed confrontation.

The most famous of these confrontations has to be the famed Battle on the Ice in 1242, in which a whole regiment of Teutonic Knights was decimated by the forces of Russian Prince Alexander Nevsky. The knights were lured out onto a frozen lake before they were hemmed in and subsequently hammered into submission by the Russian forces. A retreat was attempted, but the knights were barely able to keep from falling down on the ice in the melee. The entire affair became an utterly devastating debacle for the Teutonic Knights.

This event kept the Teutonic Knights away from the Russian frontiers. Instead, they refocused their efforts on the Baltic coast and a region known as Pomerania, which today constitutes much of Poland and part of Germany. In the same fateful year that the Battle on the Ice took place, Polish Duke Swietopelk II of Pomerania began to take issue with the Teutonic Knights stationed in the region. To get rid of them, he decided to align himself with the local warlords so that he could push them out.

In the past, the Poles had aligned themselves with the Teutonic Knights against the pagans, as was the case when the Teutonic Knights were recruited in the 1220s to aid the Poles in their struggle against the pagans of Prussia. The Teutonic Order had aligned themselves with the Polish Duke Konrad of Masovia. The Poles had recently taken a beating from Prussian warriors who had engaged in terrorist-styled attacks, killing civilians and razing religious buildings to the ground.

Prussia (not to be confused with the later Kingdom of Prussia) is yet another Baltic principality that no longer exists but, at the time, consisted of the southeastern reaches of the Baltic. The pope had famously issued a Golden Bull in regard to the Prussian attacks, sanctioning a crusade in 1230. The Teutonic Knights, the Poles, and loyal Pomeranians joined forces to slam into the pagan Prussians. The Teutonic Knights were successful in their charge and drove the Prussians out.

But every few miles the Teutonic Knights advanced, they would stop and build a fortress. By doing this, the Teutonic Knights were putting down permanent roots. Although the Polish duke was happy the Teutonic Knights helped him get rid of the Prussians, he now had to contend with a permanent army of Teutonic Knights camped out in his land.

Additionally, German immigrants from the Holy Roman Empire began to come in droves, settling the land surrounding Teutonic castles under the assumption that they were under the full protection of the Teutonic Knights. Decades later, Duke Swietopelk of Pomerania sought to remedy Poland of this situation by aligning himself with bands of Pomeranians to dispatch the Teutonic Knights.

The duke fully understood the Teutonic Knights were at their best when they could charge out of their fortresses to launch rapid strikes before returning to the refuge of their castle walls. So, the duke began to relentlessly harass and harry the knights, hoping to catch them out in the open. He led a series of successful ambush attacks, attempting to catch the knights off-guard.

Duke Swietopelk also laid siege to many of their fortresses. By 1244, the Teutonic Knights only had three fortresses left in their possession that were still fully intact. The crafty duke ended up surrounding these remaining strongholds by erecting counterforts all around the beleaguered Teutonic castles. The Teutonic Knights were able to rally their strength, and they took out the counterforts one by one.

However, in 1247, the duke had to admit that his cause was lost. At this point, the pope entered the picture, insisting the two sides come to a peaceful resolution. In 1249, the Treaty of Christburg was enacted.

Decades later, in 1308, the Teutonic Knights once again came to blows with the Polish powers, this time over the German enclave of Danzig (Poland's modern-day Gdańsk). The Teutonic Knights were victorious, but they left a veritable massacre in their wake. The devastation was apparently so bad that even the pope condemned the order. It is not known exactly how many people died, but historians agree that mass killings took place.

The Teutonic Knights would lumber on for some time, but their reputation was in shreds. This terrible event would prove to be one of the final footnotes of the Northern Crusades. Historians have deemed the Northern Crusades to be far more successful than the crusades to the Holy Land.

# Chapter 12: Crusades against Heretics

*"The surest way to work up a crusade in favor of some good cause is to promise people they will have a chance of maltreating someone. To be able to destroy with good conscience, to be able to behave badly and call your bad behavior 'righteous indignation'—this is the height of psychological luxury, the most delicious of moral treats."*

-Aldous Huxley

In this city, an offshoot of classical Christian Gnosticism managed to take root. The Christian Gnostics practiced a mystical variation of Christianity. It had first come to the forefront in the $2^{nd}$ century before it was ruthlessly suppressed by the supporters of mainstream Christianity.

The Christian Gnostics and the Cathars envisioned a world of dualism in which there was an equally good God and an equally evil one. To the Catholic Church, this seemed to be equating Satan with being somehow on par with God. This belief was considered heresy by church leaders since official Christian doctrine teaches that Satan is the fallen angel Lucifer, a being created by God. Thus, it would be logically argued that the two could not be equated. The created is not equal to the creator.

The Cathars were heavily influenced by the Gnostics who came before them. Both sects believed the world was inherently evil and that the goal of humanity was to shed their human bodies so that their souls would be free of the evil physical world. This is also contrary to church teaching since the fundamental teaching of Christianity is that the dead will be resurrected to live in a glorified (and entirely physical) body.

In the course of their religious evolution, the Cathars managed to pick up some strains of Hinduism in their teachings, as the Cathars believed in a form of reincarnation and transmigration of souls. They believed that people were continually reborn in physical form until they could finally be "freed" to roam as disembodied spirits. Such contrary teachings from those who called themselves "Christians" was more worrying to the pope than the advancing Muslim forces.

As such, a crusade was called in 1208, and the crusaders dutifully stormed into the heart of France to destroy the Cathars and those who sheltered them. Interestingly enough, this mission was considered so important that the pope's personal legate—Arnald Amalric—literally led the charge. This papal representative was on the ground, directing the carnage. Arnald Amalric wrote some rather astonishingly gleeful accounts of the bloodshed being inflicted.

At one point during the melee, he fired off a missive in which he gloated, "Today, your Holiness, twenty thousand citizens were put to the sword, regardless of age or sex." It is quite shocking to people today to hear of anyone, let alone religious leaders, casually speaking of wholesale slaughter in this fashion. But in those days, religion had become militant. Christians who were perceived to have fallen away from the mainstream faith were viewed as corrupted and akin to being a plague. It was feared that if these Christians went unchecked, their "heretical" beliefs could spread to other Christians.

In response to the news of the destruction of the Cathars, the pope wrote, "Praise and thanks to God for that which he hath mercifully wrought through thee and through these others whom zeal for the orthodox faith hath kindled to this work against his most pestilential enemies."

Here, the pope is clearly referring to the heretics as a "pestilence," as if they were some sort of virus that needed to be snuffed out. And this same mentality was in place when the Bosnian Crusade erupted in the Balkans in 1235. A hearty dose of conquest was also present, as the Kingdom of Hungary sought to add vast tracts of territory to its kingdom. This makes sense, as the leader of the Bosnian Crusade was the crown prince of Hungary, Prince Coloman.

Even though conquest was the main drive behind this crusade, religion played a role. In fact, the Bosnian Crusade was directly linked to the Albigensian Crusade, which took place years prior.

It had been rumored that a Cathar antipope named Nicetas had taken up residence in Bosnia. Today, scholars are unsure if this figure ever even existed. Nevertheless, there was very little reason to justify the terrible fighting that ensued. Beyond accusations of Bosnia harboring Nicetas, more general accusations were made that the Bosnians embraced a sect called Bogomilism. Adherents of Bogomilism believed in the duality of good and evil and were similar to the Cathars.

After all of the bloodshed ran its course, the crusaders achieved very little; they only succeeded in seizing very small sections of Bosnian territory.

The greater threat of the Mongols soon took precedence over petty squabbles among Christians. Right in the midst of the Bosnian Crusade, the Mongol armies threatened to invade the Balkans. And before it was all said and done, Prince Coloman himself would perish.

# Chapter 13: The Alexandrian and Savoyard Crusades

*"Any crusade requires optimism and the ambition to aim high."*
*-Paul Allen*

The Alexandrian Crusade, also sometimes known as the sacking of Alexandria, took place when the potentate of Cyprus, Peter I, decided it would be profitable for him to invade Alexandria, Egypt. Although often considered part of the Crusades, it has been widely noted that this particular military operation lacked much of the religious ideals that were trademarks of its predecessors.

In many ways, the Alexandrian Crusade was more or less just a preemptive strike against a foreign adversary. Peter had received some startling intelligence information indicating that the Egyptians were planning an assault on Cyprus. So, Peter raised up troops of his own to take the fight directly to Alexandria, Egypt. Peter I of Cyprus spent the better part of three years raising an army. His forces were joined by the famed Knights Hospitaller, who were holed up on the island of Rhodes.

Peter and his men met up with the knights at Rhodes in the fall of 1365. His fleet was said to have consisted of around 165 ships. The armada descended upon Alexandria on October 9th, 1365. Peter and his men stormed the city, and over the next few days, thousands were killed, and even more were taken as prisoners of war. Peter's men burned the city, razing mosques and churches alike to the ground. Egypt had—and still does have—a sizeable Christian population, but it seems even they did not fare much better than their Muslim countrymen in Peter's onslaught.

Besides robbing and murdering the inhabitants of Alexandria, Peter was apparently eager to turn the situation into another Damietta, as he believed he could use the city as a forward base for future crusades into the Middle East. But his fellow captains realized how vulnerable they were. Or perhaps they knew the history of previous ill-fated campaigns in the region. Regardless, they convinced Peter they should leave while they were still ahead.

And that was precisely what they did. Rather than sticking around to hold the city and inevitably face wrathful reinforcements, Peter's men looted as many valuables as they possibly could and killed anyone who stood in their way before hopping back onto their ships and setting sail for Cyprus. Thus, the Alexandrian Crusade is often said to be more akin to the sacking of a city than an actual ideological crusade.

But however you may quantify it, the daring raid would be remembered. It would later end up getting a mention in the famed medieval text *The Canterbury Tales*.

The Savoyard Crusade commenced on the heels of the Alexandrian Crusade. Officially sanctioned by Pope Urban V, the Savoyard Crusade was launched in the Balkans in an attempt to offset the growing threat of the Ottoman Empire. This particular crusade gets its name due to the fact that it was led by Amadeus VI, Count of Savoy.

The Savoyard Crusade saw Westerners actively collaborating with Hungary and the Byzantine Empire, the latter of which was becoming increasingly harried and hounded by the Ottomans. The pope first convinced Louis I of Hungary to take part, persuading him to take a stand against Turkish encroachment in the region. The pope was also in frequent contact with Byzantine Emperor John V Palaeologus about the terms of cooperation between the Christian West and the Christian East.

At the center of these talks were plans to heal the schism that had erupted between Latin Catholics and Orthodox Christians. The Byzantine emperor was considering reuniting with the

Catholic Church and even recognizing papal authority over the Greek Orthodox Church if he were aided in driving the Turks from the Balkans. Emperor John V seemed true to his word. In 1366, he even made his way to the court of the Hungarian king, where he swore an oath that he and his family would personally convert to Catholicism.

All of this was music to the pope's ears, and he eagerly did what he could to coordinate the crusader forces to conduct the Byzantine Empire's much-needed relief operation in the Balkans to check the expansion of the Ottoman Turks. Shortly thereafter, Amadeus led a considerable force by boat straight to the Dardanelles to attack Turkish positions in Gallipoli.

The crusaders captured the city that August after the Turks fled, and the city's residents flung open the gates. Unlike other medieval seizures of cities, the taking of Gallipoli appears to be one of liberation rather than conquest. It makes sense; this city had only recently been overrun by the Turks. The Byzantine residents certainly appreciated being rescued.

Controlling Gallipoli was of crucial importance strategically since it gave the crusaders control over what had been the main weigh station of the Turks as they crossed over into Europe. The Savoyard force reached Constantinople on September $4^{th}$, 1366, and then launched an expedition against another of Byzantium's enemies: the Bulgarians. The crusaders laid hold of the strategic settlements of Mesembria and Sozopolis that October.

The crusaders also attempted to take Varna. They hoped the citizens would just open the gates and let them in, but this was not the case. Instead, an embittered stalemate ensued.

Amadeus VI of Savoy soon found himself running out of money and was forced to return home. However, before they left, the Greeks showed their appreciation to the crusaders for aiding them against the Turks and Bulgarians. According to Savoyard chroniclers, "all orders of religion, gentlemen, citizens, merchants, people, women, and children, and [they] all went to the seaside to meet the count, crying 'Long live the count of Savoy, who has delivered Greece from the Turks and the Emperor, our Lord, from the hands of the Emperor of Bulgaria.'"

Despite all of the gratitude, the Byzantines did not convert to Catholicism, instead allowing Byzantine politics to prevail. The emperor was kind enough to fork out some fifteen thousand florins to help pay for the costs incurred by Amadeus of Savoy and his crusader force.

# Chapter 14: The Ottoman Crusades

*"The Ottoman Empire ... The rulers in Turkey were fortunately so corrupt that they left people alone pretty much. [They] were mostly interested in robbing them. And they left them alone to run their own affairs. With a lot of local self-determination."*

-*Noam Chomsky*

The Ottoman Empire, the largest contiguous empire in the history of Islam, would rise up in central Europe to shake the former giant of Asia Minor—the Byzantine Empire—to its core. The Ottomans began as various Turkic tribes that migrated into Anatolia during the tumult of Mongolian expansion. These bands of warriors eventually coalesced under one dynamic leader: Osman.

The Ottoman Empire rose up under Osman (the empire actually gets its name from Osman, whose name is Uthman in Arabic). Under Osman, the Turks struck out against the Byzantines in 1301, advancing toward Nicaea on the Byzantine Empire's southern flank. The Byzantines went into action and sent an army to intercept the intruders, but the Turks rallied and dealt the Byzantines a stunning defeat.

Many refugees poured out of Nicaea (now the Turkish city of Iznik) and fled to the higher ground of Nicomedia (the modern-day Turkish town of Izmit). The fighting would continue even after Osman perished. In 1326, the Turks managed to seize the Byzantine city of Bursa. This outpost would become the first capital city of the rapidly expanding Ottoman Empire.

The Turks would use Bursa as a forward base. They finally captured the city of Nicaea in 1331. Further advancements were made when nearby Nicomedia was taken just a few years later, in 1337. The Ottomans pushed closer and closer toward the isthmus—the thin strip of land—that connected Asia Minor to southeastern Europe, and the Byzantines seemed practically powerless to stop their advance.

The Ottomans would soon push into the Balkans and make a lasting impact on places like Serbia, Bulgaria, and Bosnia, impacts that can still be felt to this day.

In the meantime, the Byzantine Empire was in a state of panic. A disastrous conflict broke out in 1342 between two different Byzantine claimants to the throne, making matters even worse.

The drama was over the succession of a young Byzantine prince, John V Palaeologus, being contested by his regent, John Kantakozenos. During the course of the struggle, Kantakozenos became desperate enough to make friends with the Byzantine Empire's natural enemy: the Turks. He aligned himself with a Turkish warlord named Orkhan (also spelled as Orhan). With the aid of his Turkish allies, John was successful in his bid and ultimately went on to become Byzantine emperor John VI.

The Turks had greatly aided Kantakozenos in his quest, but they were now camped practically right outside of Constantinople's mighty walls. The Ottomans would continue to be enlisted as auxiliary troops, periodically fending off Bulgarian invasions. These engagements led the Turks to eventually set up camp right on the Gallipoli Peninsula. The seizure of this territory was rightfully viewed with deep suspicion by the Byzantines since it would have allowed their "allies" an easy path to strike out at the heart of the Byzantine Empire.

The situation became even worse in 1354 when an earthquake knocked down the fortified walls of several Byzantine settlements in the region. With the medieval mindset being what it was, this was not seen as a coincidence. The Turks took it as a divine invitation to seize the towns that had been "miraculously" rendered defenseless.

After this event, the Ottoman Turks were deeply rooted in what had previously been the southern heartland of the Byzantines. The Byzantines were so outraged by these developments that they seemingly placed all of the blame on the political machinations of their emperor and forced John VI Kantakozenos to resign in 1354.

About ten years later, in 1362, the Ottomans gained a powerful leader named Murad I, a figure who would serve as a unifying force for the Ottomans until his death in 1389 during the Battle of Kosovo. Murad I first began the process of utterly surrounding the Byzantine capital of Constantinople by seizing control of both sides of the isthmus on which the great metropolis sat. The Byzantines faced very little hope of succeeding on the military front, so they resorted to diplomacy and signed a treaty with the Ottoman sultan.

For a time, there would be peace, but the Byzantines were made subservient to the Ottomans and forced to pay tribute. This sense of desperation led to renewed talk in inner Byzantine circles to break out of the bind in which they found themselves.

In the meantime, the Serbs in the Balkans had grown in strength. In 1363, they managed to join forces with Hungarian, Wallachian, and Bosnian troops to wage war against Turkish positions in Adrianople. The push was successful at first, but in one of the most ridiculous reversals in history, this coalition of forces proceeded to celebrate their gains right there in the field. They camped out near the Maritza River and drank themselves into oblivion. While they were sleeping off the effects of their festivities, the Ottomans launched an assault against them. These hungover warriors were in no shape to fight and were forced to flee. Many of them perished in the process.

The Turks would solidify their gains and make Adrianople (Edirne) their official capital. It was due to all of these developments that the pope called for the Savoyard Crusade. As mentioned in the previous chapter, the Savoyard Crusade involved Duke Amadeus of Savoy, who just so happened to be the cousin of the Byzantine emperor.

The crusade was fairly successful in rolling back Turkish gains, resulting in the seizure of Gallipoli from the Turks. The Turks continued to make inroads in the Balkans, and on September 26th, 1371, they came to blows with yet another Balkan coalition led by the Serbs. This battle would go down in Turkish history as *Sirf Sindigi* ("The Destruction of the Serbs").

The name of this battle is not mere hyperbole since an army was annihilated and much of the Serbian nobility was destroyed in this catastrophic onslaught. In the aftermath, large chunks of Serbia and other Balkan territories were occupied by the Ottomans.

A champion would soon rise up in the form of Lazar of Serbia. He would attempt to push the Ottoman advance back once again. Lazar created yet another coalition, this time mostly consisting of Bulgarians, Bosnians, Serbians, Wallachians, Albanians, and Hungarians.

Murad I quickly responded to this incursion, and the two sides met for a climactic round of warfare in 1389 that would become known as the Battle of Kosovo. The Turks were once again victorious, but their victory would be bittersweet, for their leader, the great Murad I, perished.

But Murad was not killed in combat. A Serb by the name of Miloš Oblić snuck into the Ottoman encampment and assassinated Murad. After this event, Lazar of Serbia, who had been captured and made a prisoner of war during the Battle of Kosovo, was himself executed in retribution. His son, Stefan Lazarević, succeeded the throne, but he had no stomach for crusades and ultimately became an obedient puppet of the Turks while the Balkans were slowly carved up by the Ottoman state.

In 1391, the Turks seized Bosnia, and just a couple of years later, in 1393, Bulgaria found itself under Turkish dominion. With the Balkans under their thumb, the Turkish war machine then turned its attention once again to the Byzantines. Just a few years after the fall of Bulgaria, the Turks laid siege to the Byzantine city of Nicopolis and succeeded in taking it. Prince Mircea of Wallachia led a new coalition of Christian crusaders down the Danube River. They made their way to Nicopolis to face the Turks head-on.

This confrontation would later become known as the Battle of Nicopolis, which took place in 1396. The Turks had heavily fortified the city, and it soon became quite clear to the crusaders that taking it would not be an easy feat. The crusaders lacked even the most basic aspects of siege equipment.

Sultan Bayezid I, who came to the throne in 1389, had been alerted to what was happening and arrived on the scene with a formidable force. However, the Turks did not immediately attack the crusaders. Instead, they camped nearby, daring the crusaders to be the first to strike. The crusaders took the bait and soon charged right into the enemy. The strike was premature, and those who had charged headlong into the enemy found themselves in an extremely vulnerable position. The Turks were able to close in and annihilate them.

The rest of the battle was a rout, as the disorganized crusader army began to retreat in utter chaos. Most of those who fell behind were killed, but some were taken captive. Johann Schiltberger, who was a participant on the side of the crusaders, noted his version of the event.

Schiltberger stated, "Then each was ordered to kill his own prisoners, and for those who did not wish to do so, the [sultan] appointed others in their place. Then they took my companions and cut off their heads, and when it came to my turn, the [sultan's] son saw me and ordered that I should be left alive, and I was taken to the other boys, because none under 20 years of age were killed, and I was scarcely 16 years old." This testimony is indicative of the Turkish habit of sparing young men since they could be forced into serving the Ottoman army.

By this point, the situation in Constantinople was entirely untenable. The Byzantines were surrounded, and they knew their metropolis, nestled right in the midst of a vast Turkish empire, would be swallowed up soon. The Byzantine emperor actually "snuck" out of his own kingdom to make a trip to the West to plead for aid and yet another crusade.

However, no serious efforts would be made until a few decades later. Another crusading coalition was cobbled together in 1444. This time around, a scheme had been concocted to have the main vanguard of the crusader army march down the Danube River to meet the Turks while Venetian naval craft would be sent to blockade the straits, preventing reinforcements from flowing into the Balkans. And if this wasn't enough, it was planned to have the Greeks stage a diversionary attack in southern Greece.

It was believed that if all of these operations were successful, then a small group of a few thousand Turks would be left stranded in the Balkans. It would be easy for the crusaders to take down such a paltry number. It was hoped this grand strategy would succeed in driving the Turks away for good and give Constantinople some much-needed breathing space. But as they say, the best-laid plans of mice and men often go awry.

As the strategy unfolded, the Greeks did their part, creating a distraction in the Peloponnese, but the Venetians proved unable to blockade the straits of the Bosporus due to bad weather. Their ships would remain in port. The sultan's army was able to cross into the Balkans to reinforce the residual force that had been left there. This meant the crusaders faced a very large and formidable army when the two sides finally came face to face in the vicinity of Varna in November 1444.

Realizing they were grossly outnumbered, the crusaders hunkered down and literally circled their wagons as they moved into a defensive position to sustain the heavy assault that awaited them. Initially, the crusaders' tactics served them well enough. When the Turks advanced, the crusaders were able to pick quite a few of them off by launching a heavy rain of arrows in their direction.

The crusaders learned that a top Turkish commander had been killed during the first melee, which greatly heartened them. Nevertheless, the Ottomans continued their relentless advance against the beleaguered crusaders. The crusaders attempted to rally and charge their opponents but were routed in what turned into an unmitigated disaster.

In the middle of this carnage, the king of Hungary was killed. His head was placed on the tip of a spear. The Turks proudly waved this trophy high into the air for all of the crusaders to see. For them, the message was quite clear—their bold commander had fallen, and it would not be long before the rest of them would succumb as well.

Geopolitically speaking, the Greeks of the Peloponnese would suffer the most from this debacle since they were immediately subjugated and subjected to reprisals for their role in the crusade.

The Ottoman Empire was a true juggernaut and military powerhouse. It seemed as if all efforts to dislodge it would prove impossible. Nevertheless, Pope Nicholas V was ready to call for yet another crusade as a consequence of the losses that had been incurred. His biggest backer was George Skanderbeg of Albania.

This leading figure of Christendom cobbled together a suitable force of crusaders, but in doing so, he incurred the wrath of Sultan Murad II, who immediately struck out at Albania. Hungary's crusading champion John Hunyadi and a coalition of Hungarians and Wallachians sent troops to aid the beleaguered Albanians. The forces then collided in Kosovo, leading to the 1448 Second Battle of Kosovo.

The crusade would meet its end here, as it was a decisive Ottoman victory. The Turks were able to consolidate their gains in the Balkans and turn their focus toward toppling the Byzantine Empire.

This feat was achieved just a few years later by Murad II's son, Mehmed II. After a protracted siege, Constantinople fell to the Ottoman Turks in 1453. It was pleas from Constantinople that had kickstarted the Crusades in the first place, and now the once-mighty Christian capital of the East had fallen. The shock of Constantinople's fall was profound, not only to Christendom but also to the world.

# Chapter 15: The Reconquista— Setting the Stage for Things to Come

*"The Sultan Abd-er-Rahman was one of the Heaven-sent rulers of men. Prompt yet cautious in council and in war, unscrupulous, overbearing and proud, he was as ready to wreak terrible vengeance, as he was politic to forgive when it suited him. Berber and Yamanite alike acknowledged that at last they had found their master. He ruled until his death, in 788, with the tempered severity, wisdom, and justice which made his domain the best organized in Europe, and his capital the most splendid in the world."*

-*S. P. Scott*

The Iberian Peninsula stands as one of the most unique geographical regions in the crusading period. As mentioned earlier, the Visigothic Christian kings ruled Spain in the early 700s, but they began to be harassed and harried by Islamic forces arriving from North Africa. It was just a hop, skip, and jump to cross the Strait of Gibraltar and lay siege to the southern beaches of Spain. And during this period, the assaults were happening more and more frequently.

All of this led to a massive incursion by a Muslim warlord whose name comes down to us as Tariq in 711 CE. Tariq's forces were victorious. They crushed the Visigoths and took over nearly all of the Iberian Peninsula. The invaders even pushed into France until they were stopped by the mighty ruler known as the Hammer—Charles Martel (better known as Charlemagne).

Back in conquered Iberia, the entire peninsula had been overrun, save for the remote mountainous enclaves where a Christian resistance was kept on life support. However, this small Christian holdout would one day march forth from the corner it had been backed into and revive Christian Iberia (which its Muslim conquerors referred to as al-Andalus).

In the first stages of the conquest, al-Andalus was overseen by administrators who hailed from the Umayyad dynasty, which was based out of Damascus, Syria. The Umayyads were overthrown and displaced by another group, the Abbasids, in the 740s, which changed the course of Iberian history. For one thing, the capital of the Abbasid dynasty was Baghdad, Iraq. This meant those who were tasked with running the Iberian Peninsula were quite far from the peninsula itself.

The drama between the Abbasids and the Umayyads was not yet over, though. Even though the ruthless Abbasids had killed much of the former Umayyad nobility in their pursuit of power, a young prince by the name of Abd al-Rahman had escaped their clutches. Like a king in exile, Rahman grew up with a fire in his belly and a determination in his heart to take back his kingdom.

He eventually made his way to Córdoba, Spain, in 756, where he declared himself to be a sovereign ruler of an independent Umayyad state. Perhaps considering how brutal (as well as apathetic due to their faraway administrative posts in Baghdad) the Abbasids had been, the residents of Iberia jumped at the chance to rally behind Abd al-Rahman. The Abbasids apparently did not put up much resistance to this takeover (if they noticed at all), and Iberia remained an independent emirate for a time.

Eventually, those tasked with running al-Andalus would find the greatest danger they faced was not from rival Muslim powers but from the Christian enclaves in the northern mountains. They had been patiently waiting for just the right time to come down and take back what had once belonged to them.

A ruthless Muslim leader who seized power in al-Andalus took center stage of this struggle in the 980s. His name comes down to us as al-Mansur. He proved himself to be an excellent military strategist and managed to keep the Christians in the north in check. He also gained ground on the North African coast of Morocco.

Al-Mansur's rule was essentially a dictatorship, and while he was crushing external enemies, he was also quelling internal opponents. He managed to clean house so thoroughly that he decimated the internal bureaucratic machinery that had allowed the Muslims to control Iberia efficiently. Al-Mansur would pass away in 1002, leaving a corrupt and chaotic legacy of governance in his wake. The name given to this period was *fitna*, which means "anarchy."

Al-Andalus went from a united peninsula, with territories spilling into North Africa, to several warlord states. The division of al-Andalus would be crucial for the Christian reconquest of the peninsula since it was much easier to take a piece of Spain back at a time. Toppling minor kingdoms was an easier goal than standing up to a united and powerful peninsula-wide regime.

Interestingly enough, many of the weaker warlord states realized just how precarious of a situation they were in and began paying tribute to some of the most powerful Christian kings in northern Iberia to keep them from attacking.

As the Christians' foes became more fractured, the two Christian powers of León and Castile merged together when Ferdinand the Great of Castile wed the sister (and ultimately the heir) of the king of León. Due to the tribute they received from Muslim states, León and Castile began to slowly become quite wealthy. Rather than being vagabond kings hiding in the wilderness, these Christian states grew financially and militarily strong.

But these petty warlords soon began to groan under the strain of the *fitna* system. After the Christians seized control of Toledo, they finally sought help. In what was essentially an Islamic call for a crusade against the Christians, aid was requested from the powerful Almoravids, who had taken over Morocco. In 1086–

about a decade prior to Urban II's first call for a Christian crusade—the Almoravids sailed to Iberia and engaged the Iberian Christians in battle.

The Islamic forces scored a victory, and the Christian troops were driven out. The Almoravids quickly realized the weakness of the fractured system that had existed in Iberia and attempted to reinstate a more unified form of governance. But it did not last. In just a matter of years, the Almoravids were losing power, and around 1120, they had to concede defeat and give up al-Andalus outright.

The Christian kingdoms were on the rise and began to unite increasingly more with each other. León and Castile were ultimately absorbed by a rising power known as the Kingdom of Pamplona. After Pamplona gained the Kingdom of Aragon, it became the much larger Principality of Catalonia.

However, at the dawning of the 1100s, the kingdom retracted, and Navarre became the main focal point of Christian Iberia. During the Second Crusade in the 1140s, the pope took notice of what was happening in Iberia and coordinated to have significant manpower sent to the peninsula.

At the behest of Alfonso I Henriques of Portugal, Flemish soldiers and a batch of Anglo-Norman warriors, who were on their way to the Holy Land, made a pit stop in Iberia. They joined forces with the Portuguese to seize the important Iberian port city (and ultimately the capital of Portugal), Lisbon.

Although much of the Second Crusade is remembered as a dismal failure, this side mission proved to be a stunning success. Lisbon was ultimately reclaimed for Christendom on October $24^{th}$, 1147. Christian knights continued to be summoned to Iberia to support the reconquest of vast tracts of land. These lands began to define the boundaries of what would become Portugal and Spain.

One interesting development was the establishment of a unique Iberian monastic order of knights, which would become known as the Order of Santiago. Santiago is actually the Spanish name for Saint James. It was believed the remains of Saint James had been miraculously discovered in northern Spain.

According to Catholic tradition, James had conducted missionary work in Spain before heading back to Jerusalem to lead the early church. Since James's alleged visit is not mentioned in scripture, it is not entirely clear where this account comes from. However, the Bible documents that James was in Jerusalem when he was martyred. The Spanish legend insists that his body was shipped off to Spain.

This order of knights would often be on the frontlines of the conflict to reconquer Iberia. Prior to Iberian-based orders, the Knights Templar had some limited participation in the region, but it proved much more practical to have monastic orders native to the peninsula to permanently safeguard the gains being made in the Reconquista.

The southward push against the Muslim settlements continued, resulting in a major exchange between Christian and Muslim forces in 1195 at the Battle of Alarcos. At the fortress of Alarcos, the beaten and battered Castilian troops sought refuge. In the end, the Castilians had to admit defeat and surrender, which led to the loss of several strategic fortresses and further incursions by their adversary.

But even so, just a couple of years later, in 1212, another tremendous battle between the two sides was waged in Iberia. The Battle of Las Navas de Tolosa would completely alter the course of history.

A force led by the unified Spanish kingdoms of Castile, Aragon, and Navarre hooked up with a contingent of Portuguese troops and delivered their opponents a stunning blow. Prior to this, Muslim forces had regained some territory and appeared to be on the rise. After this major defeat, though, much of their gains would be lost.

Most historians believe the Battle of Las Navas de Tolosa was the turning point for the entire Reconquista. After this decisive victory, Christian forces were able to push farther south. As it pertains to the Portuguese, a rapid advance to the Algarve region in 1249 led to the complete seizure of the territory that would come to define modern-day Portugal.

However, not all of these territorial gains went without their moment of controversy. One must consider how difficult it would have been for some of these Christian kings to determine who would get what. As it turns out, the king of Castile was not happy with the Portuguese claims in the Algarve, leading to a lengthy dispute between the two powers.

The pope proved to be a useful diplomat in this disagreement, as he diffused a potentially deadly dispute through negotiations. The Treaty of Alcañices was signed in the year 1297. It was in this treaty that the exact boundaries between Castile and Portugal would be sorted out.

This mediation by the pope set a precedent that would be followed in later years. The papacy would again play the vital role of mediator when Portugal and Spain divvied up much of the New World (the Americas) between each other.

As the Spanish and Portuguese reclaimed their territory in Iberia, the Muslim settlements in the peninsula were being squeezed more and more until they were pigeonholed into the southernmost enclaves of the Iberian Peninsula. Soon, all that would remain of al-Andalus was just one southern corner of Iberia, which would become known as Granada.

The Christian expansion would not go unanswered. A new Muslim power from North Africa, the Marinids, would arrive on the scene. The Marinids showed up around the year 1275 and offered their aid to the besieged region of Granada. Their aid was not always appreciated by the Granadans, though. As was the case before, when "outside help" arrived, there was almost certainly disruption and oppression at the local level.

After the Marinids arrived to strengthen the position of the enclave, the Christian kings came to realize the importance of gaining control of the narrow strait that flowed between the North African coast and the southern tip of Spain. Until the connection between Granada and the North African coast was severed, there would always be a threat of incursions and reinforcements being sent from Muslim strongholds in Morocco. As such, securing the strait became the Christians' main objective.

The Christian kingdoms of Iberia waged war against the Marinid newcomers. In 1292, the Christians managed to seize Tarifa. Then, in 1310, even greater success occurred with the seizure of Gibraltar. Gibraltar is the island that lies in the strait between North Africa and Spain. It was a convenient stop for invasion forces and was of strategic importance for the Christian kings. The Christians temporarily lost Gibraltar in the back-and-forth struggle that followed, but by 1350, the Christian dominance of the strait was complete. Grenada was effectively surrounded with no hope of reinforcements.

In the end, it would be the mighty Spanish power couple of Ferdinand II of Aragon and Isabella I of Castile who managed to seize Granada in 1491. They finished the Reconquista, securing the entire Iberian Peninsula in 1492. And as anyone who has ever read a history book might know, that fateful year of 1492 saw a man named Christopher Columbus sail the ocean blue on behalf of the Spanish Crown.

Although Columbus didn't realize it at the time, he had stumbled upon a whole new continent. And since the victorious armies of Christian Europe had finished the Reconquista, they were looking for something new to do. Heading to the New World and conquering it for their countries sounded appealing.

But why did Columbus even sail westward? Well, the fall of Constantinople and the subsequent closure of the old roads to the East led Columbus and other explorers to look for an alternate route to India. Columbus believed India could be found by sailing westward, but he accidentally "discovered" the Americas (for those who don't know, Leif Erikson was the first European to discover the Americas, although native tribes had lived there even before Erikson made his journey).

The Crusades and the Reconquista were also major factors in exploring the New World. The Portuguese and Spaniards had spent centuries trying to reclaim Iberia, so they had become understandably militant about their faith. They had fought hundreds of years of religious wars. With this in mind, it is easier to understand the mindset conquistadors had when confronted with the Maya, Aztecs, and Inca, civilizations that had not been introduced to the Christian God.

When the Spanish conquistador Hernán Cortés beheld the Aztecs conducting human sacrifices, with Aztec priests ripping out the hearts of their sacrificial victims, his reaction was both understandable and predictable. The Spaniards and Portuguese were determined to conquer this new land for Christ, just as they had done in Iberia.

For better or for worse, these battle-hardened Christian crusaders, riding high on the waves of the victorious conclusion of Iberia's Reconquista, were ready to stake their claims in the New World. As much as we tend to condemn these men today (and there is certainly plenty of reason to do so), one can only imagine what might have occurred if the forces of Islam were the victors rather than the Christians. If that were the case, would a Muslim version of Columbus have sailed from the Islamic stronghold of Iberia and discovered the New World? Would the armies of Islam have given the Native Americans a choice—submit to Islam or go to war? Rather than having a staunchly Catholic Mexico, Cuba, Colombia, and Brazil, would these countries have mosques on every corner?

So, what is the point of mentioning all this? The point is that those who engaged in the Reconquista were militant, brutal, and aggressive, but they were no more so than their Islamic opponents. It is impossible to say for sure, but if the Muslims were the ones to travel to the New World, their conquest of the Americas would have likely resulted in the same dislocation of Native American civilizations. It is safe to say, though, that much blood has been spilled in the name of religion throughout history.

# Conclusion: The Lasting Legacy of the Crusades

Whether we like it or not, the Crusades are a crucial lynchpin in history. Without them, the world today would be a much different place. As much as we might be tempted to demonize one side, we are missing the bigger picture if we do. The Crusades were not launched on the mere whims of some pope who wanted to be mean and nasty and colonize the Middle East. The Crusades were a defensive operation aimed at aiding the Greek Byzantines.

And whether we agree with it or not, the subsequent seizure of the Holy Land was also viewed as a kind of Reconquista since all of the Levant had been controlled by Christians until it was forcibly seized by the forces of Islam in the $7^{th}$ century. By the time of the Crusades, the question of who had control of these lands was seen through the brutal lens of the Middle Ages, in which property rights fell to whoever was willing to fight for them.

If a clear and balanced portrayal of the Crusades and what led up to them were presented, we would see that both sides used the same fanatical ideology to justify their uncompromising brutality. There were no "good guys" and "bad guys" in these religious wars. Each side thought they were justified. And more often than not, each side felt the ends justified the means. This is indeed the ultimate legacy of what would become known as the Crusades.

Here's another book by Enthralling History that you might like

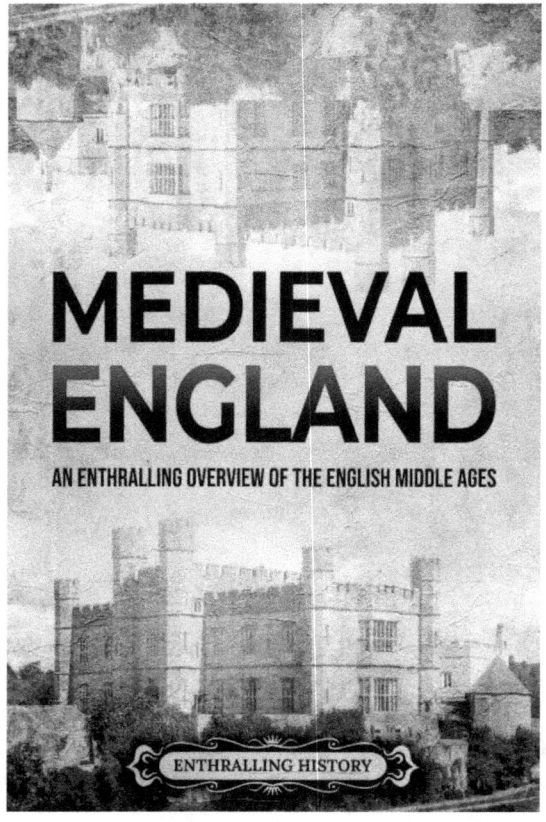

## Free limited time bonus

Stop for a moment. We have a free bonus set up for you. The problem is this: we forget 90% of everything that we read after 7 days. Crazy fact, right? Here's the solution: we've created a printable, 1-page pdf summary for this book that you're reading now. All you have to do to get your free pdf summary is to go to the following website:

https://livetolearn.lpages.co/enthrallinghistory/

Once you do, it will be intuitive. Enjoy, and thank you!

# Appendix A: Further Reading and Reference

Disney, Anthony. R. *A History of Portugal and the Portuguese Empire.* 2007.

Ellul, Max. *The Sword and the Green Cross: The Saga of the Knights of Saint Lazarus from the Crusades to the 21$^{st}$ Century.* 2011.

Madden, Thomas. *Crusades: The Illustrated History.* 2002.

Murray, Alan. *The Crusades: An Encyclopedia.* 2008.

Riley-Smith, Jonathan. *The Knights Hospitaller: In the Levant, c. 1070-1309.* 2012.

Turnbull, Stephen. *The Ottoman Empire: 1326-1699.* 2003.

www.ingramcontent.com/pod-product-compliance
Lightning Source LLC
Chambersburg PA
CBHW070340010526
44107CB00004B/573